# COLLABORATIVE APPROACHES TO LEARNING FOR PUPILS WITH PDA

*by the same authors*

**Can I tell you about Pathological Demand Avoidance syndrome?**
A guide for friends, family and professionals
*Ruth Fidler and Phil Christie*
*Illustrated by Jonathon Powell*
ISBN 978 1 84905 513 0
eISBN 978 0 85700 929 6
Part of the 'Can I tell you about...?' series

**Understanding Pathological Demand Avoidance Syndrome in Children**
A Guide for Parents, Teachers and Other Professionals
*Phil Christie, Margaret Dunn, Ruth Fidler and Zara Healy*
ISBN 978 1 84905 074 6
eISBN 978 0 85700 253 2
Part of the 'JKP Essentials' series

# COLLABORATIVE APPROACHES TO LEARNING FOR PUPILS WITH PDA

## Strategies for Education Professionals

## RUTH FIDLER
## and PHIL CHRISTIE

Jessica Kingsley *Publishers*
London and Philadelphia

Figure 8.2 The Engagement Profile contains public sector information licensed under the Open Government Licence v3.0.

First published in 2019
by Jessica Kingsley Publishers
73 Collier Street
London N1 9BE, UK
and
400 Market Street, Suite 400
Philadelphia, PA 19106, USA

*www.jkp.com*

**Library of Congress Cataloging in Publication Data**
A CIP catalog record for this book is available from the Library of Congress

**British Library Cataloguing in Publication Data**
A CIP catalogue record for this book is available from the British Library

ISBN 978 1 78592 017 2
eISBN 978 1 78450 261 4

Printed and bound by CPI Group (UK) Ltd, Croydon, CR0 4YY

# Contents

# INTRODUCTION

As we were in the process of writing this text a report was published by the All Party Parliamentary Group on Autism (APPGA 2017) on how the education system works for children and young people on the autism spectrum. This report was highly critical of the experience provided for many children, young people and their families in terms of getting an appropriate assessment and finding the right school place. It described how, for some children, 'their educational experience becomes a pathway for failure' (p.31). The report found that fewer than half of children with autism said they were happy at school and that the same number said that their teachers didn't know how to support them. The recommendations included that autism understanding should be embedded in the education system and that there should be a specialist curriculum for all pupils who need one.

The focus of this book is on a group of children who may fit the profile described as pathological demand avoidance (PDA), which is now widely understood to be a profile within the autism spectrum. The book is intended for educational practicioners who might be working with children across different ages and in the full range of educational settings. Our own experience has been developed from working within and leading a specialist autism provision, from providing training and consultancy in connection with pupils in diverse provisions and from working with parents who are often struggling to find the best way to widen educational opportunities and experiences for their children.

What this experience has underlined for us is that there are a number of children who have these complex difficulties in social understanding, communication and behaviour who seem to need more flexibility and negotiation, and a less direct style than is typically the case with other children on the autism spectrum.

The children who need this more collaborative approach to learning and teaching typically have very high levels of anxiety and find it hard to tolerate the demands and expectations of other people. They are also often adept at avoiding these 'perceived demands' and are controlling of other people and aspects of their environment. They may have received a diagnosis that includes a reference to pathological demand avoidance or a 'demand avoidant profile'. They may, though, not have received this sort of diagnosis but be displaying a behavioural profile that resonates with parents or teachers who have come across accounts of PDA.

Throughout the book there are examples given from our work with children and young people with PDA and their families and schools. Most of these will have come from assessments carried out at the Elizabeth Newson Centre or when we were involved as school leaders at the associated specialist school for children with autism. Others have been taken from our subsequent consultancy work. All examples have been anonymised. Templates of the forms used can be downloaded at www.jkp.com/catalogue/book/9781785920172 for use in your own assessments.

We are particularly grateful for the help provided by Suzanne Farrell, who is our colleague at Autism Associates with a background in curriculum and assessment. Suzanne has made a significant contribution to Chapters 6 and 8 which reflect those issues.

## Chapter 1

# TOWARDS AN
# UNDERSTANDING OF PDA

This book is not intended to give a full account of the continuing debate, discussion and controversies that exist around the PDA profile and where precisely it fits within the systems of diagnostic classification. Those who are interested in thinking about this further can follow up through the references given for this chapter. It is, though, helpful to have a short overview of the clinical and research developments that have contributed to an emerging understanding of the characteristic diagnostic profile and the issues that have arisen from this work.

Pathological demand avoidance (PDA) was a term first used by Professor Elizabeth Newson in the early 1980s. The initial descriptions of this profile were introduced in a series of lectures, presentations and papers that described a gradually developing understanding of a group of children who had been referred for diagnostic assessment at the clinic she led at the Child Development Research Unit of Nottingham University. Most of the children referred to the clinic were complex and unusual in their developmental profile and many reminded the referring professionals of children with autism or Asperger syndrome. At the same time, though, they were often seen as 'atypical' in some ways.

Newson, and the colleagues she worked with, felt increasingly dissatisfied with the description of 'atypical autism', a term that was used quite widely at the time. They felt that it was not particularly helpful in removing the confusion that was often felt by parents and teachers who were struggling to gain greater insight into the child's behaviour. As time went by, it became apparent that, while these children were indeed 'atypical' of the understandings of autism or Asperger syndrome at the time, they were very *similar to each other* in some very important ways. The central feature that was characteristic of all the children was 'an obsessional avoidance of the ordinary demands of everyday life' (Newson, Le Marechal and David 2003, p.596). This was combined with sufficient social understanding and sociability to enable the child to be 'socially manipulative' in their avoidance. Newson proposed that PDA should be seen as 'a separate syndrome within the Pervasive Developmental Disorders' (p.596), which was the recognised category used within the versions of the psychiatric classification systems that were current at the time (ICD-10, World Health Organization 1992, and DSM-IV, American Psychiatric Association 1994).

Newson's work on PDA attracted great interest as well as a degree of controversy. This continues to be the case today. At the centre of the interest has been the strong sense of recognition, expressed by both parents and professionals, of the developmental and behavioural profile that she so clearly described. Parents, in particular, recounted a 'light bulb moment' on reading the accounts and a feeling that they were, at last, hearing a description that seemed to make sense of their child. The controversy that arose was about whether PDA existed as a separate syndrome within the pervasive developmental disorders or whether the behaviours could be explained within other diagnostic categories. This debate continues today and research carried out over the last few years is helping to clarify the situation.

In the years following Newson et al.'s 2003 publication, the first paper on PDA to appear in a peer-reviewed journal, it became apparent that the term 'autism spectrum disorder' (ASD) was being used as though it was the same as pervasive developmental disorder. In fact, the National Autism Plan for Children, also published in 2003, talked about the term 'ASD' 'broadly coinciding with the term Pervasive Developmental Disorder' (p.16). The more recently published National Institute for Health and Clinical Excellence (NICE) guidelines on autism spectrum disorders (2011) described the two terms as being 'synonymous'.

The importance of this is that PDA is now widely considered to be part of the autism spectrum, or one of the autism spectrum conditions. This view was endorsed when the National Autistic Society (NAS) updated their website in 2015 to include information about PDA as a profile within the autism spectrum (NAS n.d.).

## What are the characteristic features of the PDA profile?

Individuals with PDA share difficulties with other people on the autism spectrum in terms of social aspects of interaction and communication, together with some repetitive patterns of behaviour. Children and young people with PDA often seem to have better social understanding than others on the spectrum, which means some of their difficulties may be less obvious at first. They are also able to use social strategies in attempts to avoid demands in a way that Elizabeth Newson described as 'socially manipulative' but others tend to describe as socially 'strategic' (O'Nions, Happé and Viding 2016). It is important to remember that PDA is dimensional and affects individuals to a varying extent and interacts with other factors such as their personality, intelligence and circumstances.

PDA is best understood as an anxiety-driven need to be in control and avoid other people's demands and expectations. Demand avoidance can, of course, be seen in the development of a number of children. It is the *extent* and *extreme* nature of this avoidance that causes such difficulties, which is why it has been described as 'pathological'.

The main features of PDA as they appear in children are given below.

### Resisting and avoiding the ordinary demands of life

It is this feature of behaviour that gives the name to the condition. Children can seem under an extraordinary degree of pressure from everyday expectations and they may attempt to avoid these to a remarkable extent. These demands include everyday trivial expectations such as a suggestion that it's time to get up, go out of the house or join a family activity. At times, *any* suggestion made by another person can be perceived as a demand and cause extreme levels of anxiety. This may be the case even when the child seems to want to do what has been suggested or when the request is within their capability.

Isaac Russell has produced a video extract where he talks about his experience of PDA. This can be accessed through a link on the PDA Society website as 'My experience of PDA' (www.pdasociety.org.uk/resources/webinars). Isaac, who attends a specialist setting for children with autism, was asked to describe his feelings of anxiety.

I feel most anxious when I'm being pressed to do something that I feel I can't do but the people around me don't understand me when I say I can't do that because it seems such an easy thing...they'd be able to do it, why can't I?... They keep pressing me because it seems like it would be easy. That's when I feel most anxious.

For example, if I'm having a really, really difficult day and I feel like I can leave the house but only if I don't wear shoes and someone says, 'Well you can't go out...you have to wear shoes,' and I sort of go, 'Well I can't'...it seems like I should be able to...I know how to put shoes on but there's still part of me that's going 'No, I can't do that...I cant do that.' It's that part of me, that controls...that's the person driving my brain and that at that moment that's so difficult to communicate. I know that it's stupid that I should be able to put my shoes on, but at the same time, *I can't*, I just can't. That's really difficult to deal with because its difficult to explain to other people around you, it's difficult to come to terms with yourself because how do you know things on one level but still be unable to comprehend it on another? It's such a juxtaposition...that's why it's difficult to understand PDA because it feels like it should be something that's easy but it's not.

A key feature of PDA is that the child has sufficient social understanding to use social strategies and what Elizabeth Newson described as a level of 'social manipulation' in these attempts, and will often adapt strategies to the person making the demand.

These can include:

- distracting the adult

- acknowledging the demand but giving an excuse about why they can't, for example, 'I'm sorry, I'm tired, my legs don't work'

- procrastination and negotiation

- physically incapacitating themselves, for example by not moving

- withdrawing into fantasy

- physical outbursts or attacks.

Oscar uses a range of avoidance strategies to delay an activity or to try to refuse to do what he is asked. For example, if asked to put his shoes on, he makes excuses such as, 'I don't know where my shoes are' and, when told they are in the hall, 'I don't know where the hall is.' If given his shoes he will say, 'I can't put them on my feet – I can't close them.' If asked to get something from his room he will say, 'I don't know where my room is.' He will 'lie' when asked if he has brushed his teeth, saying, 'I've brushed my teeth already.' He will also say, 'I can't be good. I can't be good,' and even, 'I'm not Oscar.' His parents feel that he tries to distract them 'endlessly' and that there is this feeling of 'continual negotiation'. By the time they have got to the end of the discussion they have forgotten what they wanted him to do. He has a wide repertoire of such tactics.

Those with PDA may also use straightforward refusal or outbursts of explosive behaviour, including aggression. This is a form of panic on their part and is usually displayed when other strategies haven't worked or when their anxiety is too high that they will 'explode' or have a 'meltdown'. This can take the form of shouting, screaming, throwing things and physically lashing out, often in very sudden and dramatic ways, with little regard for how others may perceive their behaviour.

### Appearing sociable on the surface but lacking depth in their understanding

Children with PDA often appear sociable at first, seek out interaction and seem 'people orientated'. They have often learned many social niceties and may decline a request or suggestion politely. They usually seem well tuned in to what might prove effective as a strategy with a particular person. They sometimes appear as overconfident, socially, which masks their difficulties with anxiety and judging what is socially appropriate in a given situation.

It becomes apparent that their social responses are unsubtle and lack real depth. They can be misleading and overpowering, and may overreact to seemingly trivial events. Children with PDA have difficulty seeing boundaries, accepting social obligation and taking responsibility for their actions.

Individuals with PDA often fail to understand the unwritten social boundaries or divides that exist between adults and children. They can become overfamiliar or come across as 'bossy'. They also seem to lack a sense of pride or embarrassment and can behave in very uninhibited ways:

> When observed during her assessment it became clear that Joanne had a need to control both people and situations around her. Although she was happy to play with Cathy (the psychologist), this was only when the play was based on her terms. For example, when she was playing with the dressing-up clothes and Cathy walked over and asked if she could dress up too, Joanne said, 'No, you can't.' Eventually Joanne said that she would allow Cathy to dress up, but only if she wore what she told her to: the 'sparkly' jacket.

In another assessment Claire's mum went on to describe how:

> Claire won't take responsibility for her own actions and has 'no cut-off point' in terms of her challenging behaviour. A recent example was when Claire kicked her mum in the back but didn't seem to realise that she had hurt her. She feels that Claire has a very poorly developed sense of social empathy and no true sense of the impact of her behaviour on others. Claire's teacher feels that she knows the theory behind empathy but doesn't apply it.

## Displaying excessive mood swings and impulsivity

Children with PDA can switch from one mood to another very suddenly in a way that can be described as 'like switching a light on and off'. The emotions shown may seem very dramatic and 'over the top'. As well as experiencing sudden 'spikes' in excitement or anger they may also have sudden drops in their mood. On some days children will be more sensitive and 'spiky' than others according to their level of anxiety.

Difficulty with regulating emotions is common in all children on the autism spectrum, but is especially prevalent in PDA. Mood swings and impulsivity also persist beyond childhood in the majority of those with PDA. This switching of mood often seems to be driven by the child's need to control and makes children with PDA very unpredictable.

Thinking about this in the context of the classroom, or at home, it is important to consider how this impacts on the adult. If the child suddenly becomes very agitated or excited, for example, this inevitably has the effect of raising the emotional arousal of the adult. The child might then revert to a more level state, much more quickly than the adult who is trying to support them. Recognising and being aware of this 'mismatch' in mood is important.

### Being comfortable in role play and pretend, sometimes to an extreme extent

Children with PDA are often highly interested in role play and pretend. This was recognised early on as having a different quality from that of other children on the autism spectrum. Children with PDA often mimic and take on the roles of others, extending and taking on their style, not simply repeating and re-enacting what they may have heard or seen in a repetitive or echoed way. Children with PDA can be very controlling of the play of their peers or adults who try to join in and will direct the 'script'. They will also often incorporate role play or pretend in the strategies that they use to avoid demands or exercise control.

Some children with PDA can become so involved and engrossed in their pretend worlds that the boundaries between what is real and what is fantasy become blurred. This can present issues in their developing sense of identity and self-awareness.

During Gemma's assessment she seemed to become absorbed in her role play, and it often was unclear when she was herself, or a character. She was highly expressive during this time, both in her voice and her actions. For example, she sometimes spoke in an American accent, and used some borrowed phrases such as TTYL (talk to you later). She also declared, 'We are going to see the *movie* of the *century!*' and punctuated these words with exaggerated hand gestures. During this time, Gemma did not include Cathy (psychologist) in her play, and it seemed as if she desired an audience rather than someone to play with. She gave excuses to avoid Cathy's input into her play, and often changed her story mid-sentence to support why they would not work. For example, when Cathy suggested they play charades before her 'date', she protested she did not have enough time – 'My car only goes two miles per hour' – and that she had to 'stop to get sweets'.

### Displaying 'obsessive' behaviour that is often focused on other people

This characteristic is common across all children on the autism spectrum. Newson noted that the demand avoidant behaviour itself usually has an 'obsessive' feel.

Children on the autism spectrum characteristically develop special interests, which often focus on factual information or collections of one sort. Children with PDA frequently have a strong fascination with pretend characters and scenarios or 'fixations' which often revolve around specific individuals they interact with. This can result in blame, victimisation and harassment that cause problems with peer relationships.

Jane Sherwin writes about her daughter Mollie in her book about parenting a child with PDA (2015, p.31) and describes how she 'became obsessed with her friend Gemma…treating her as if she were her child. She tried to control Gemma's every move and keep her isolated from the group…one particular meltdown at school happened because Gemma refused to use the toilet she had told her to use.'

### Other considerations

Developing clinical and research work continues to refine our understanding of these features as diagnostic criteria: how exactly they present in individuals, which features are primary and which might be secondary and how the features may overlap in those children with other conditions. Elizabeth Newson's early work also described the fact that many children with PDA have elements of clumsiness and 'neurological involvement' but this isn't the case with all. There are also a high proportion who are *delayed in some aspect of their early speech and language development*, although this may be dependent on their overall intellectual ability. Where this does occur, the initial delay seems to be part of an overall passivity and there is often a sudden degree of catch-up.

Individuals with PDA have more fluent use of eye contact and conversational timing than others on the autism spectrum. Generally, they tend to have less difficulty understanding non-verbal communication.

While the majority of those with PDA become fluent in using expressive language, some have a problem with their understanding. They can have difficulty with processing what they hear and need additional time to do this. This can lead to misunderstandings and disruption to the communication process which can contribute to their behaviour. This apparent fluency can also lead to children with PDA being 'missed' or misdiagnosed when clinicians are looking for a more typical ASD presentation of characteristics.

## Recent research and developments

In 2011 the NAS and the Elizabeth Newson Centre worked collaboratively to hold the first in what has become a series of national conferences on PDA, which have included presentations covering research, diagnosis, education and family support needs. At this conference, Francesca Happé, Professor of Cognitive Neuroscience at the Institute of Psychiatry, talked about the quality and detail of the clinical accounts of PDA and the strong recognition factor amongst parents and teachers. She went on to say that there was a real need to underpin this with empirical research. Since then Liz O'Nions, working with Francesca Happé and others, including Essie Vidings, Judy Gould and Christopher Gilberg, has carried out a number of studies that have culminated in several articles being published (e.g. O'Nions *et al.* 2014; 2016a). One of these (O'Nions *et al.* 2014) describes the development and preliminary validation of the Extreme Demand Avoidance Questionnaire (EDA-Q), which has the potential to quantify PDA traits to assist in the identification and differentiation of this group for further research. This is not a validated diagnostic tool but can nonetheless be used as a guide to identify possibile PDA traits and provide helpful input to forming a clearer picture of a child.

Another study (O'Nions *et al.* 2016) looked at the Diagnostic Interview for Social and Communication Disorders (DISCO), which was developed by Lorna Wing, Judy Gould and colleagues (2002). The DISCO is a semi-structured interview widely used as an assessment tool for autism spectrum disorders. The original assessment included some items relevant to PDA and a later extension to the instrument included a 15-item list to capture Newson's descriptions. O'Nions *et al.* (2016a) endorsed 11 of these items as being commonly observed in individuals reported to have PDA. They were also found to be relatively unusual in the autism spectrum in general and therefore potentially helpful in differentiating children with PDA diagnostically.

The research is now developing tools that can reliably be used by others wanting to carry out further work and which may offer a starting point for developing clinical guidelines and instruments. It is also suggesting that the features of PDA are dimensional across the autism spectrum and across a range of severity. Where a constellation of features appears at sufficient intensity and frequency the PDA profile is recognised. There is also a more balanced gender ratio in PDA compared to within the autism spectrum more generally.

We have made the point in earlier publications (Christie 2007; Christie *et al.* 2012) that the ongoing controversy about the use of the term 'PDA' and how it relates to those in the diagnostic classification systems can serve as a distraction, and that the focus should be on how a diagnostic understanding of an individual can help to formulate more effective forms of support and management. This view has been supported recently by O'Nions *et al.* (2016a) in their article for the DECP Debate issue of the British Psychological Society Division of Educational and Clinical Psychologists. In this paper they conclude the following:

> Children who exhibit this very problematic behavioural profile need to have their difficulties in complying with demands and extreme/controlling behaviour fully addressed in assessments, as it is these behaviours that typically create the most challenge for families and schools. Appropriate description and formulation of the child's difficulties is the starting point for the identification of potential management strategies and appropriate educational support. It is essential that help is provided for these very vulnerable children and their families. (p.iii)

## Implications for education professionals

The first accounts of PDA resonated strongly with a large number of teachers and other professionals who were finding that many of the tried and tested 'autism strategies' were proving less effective for children with the PDA profile. Newson and colleagues had started to outline some of the key differences by producing the first 'Education and Handling Guidelines' (1998) that promoted an approach based on being less directive and more flexible than the more structured methods usually advocated for children with autism. These guidelines have since been rewritten and adopted as part of the National Autism Standards, published by the Autism Education Trust (Jones *et al.* 2012).

In our earlier book (*Understanding Pathological Demand Avoidance Syndrome in Children*, Christie *et al.* 2012) we were able to outline and extend some of these flexible, indirect approaches in a chapter on positive everyday strategies. We also described, in another chapter, the importance of working with children and young people to build their self-awareness and emotional resilience to enable them to better understand and regulate their own anxiety and emotions. In this book we are able to take these ideas further and give more practical examples for teachers and other educational practicioners. We have described the key principles and strategies as 'Collaborative Approaches to Learning'.

Before going on to look at these principles and strategies in detail we want to think a bit more about the implications of the PDA profile, both from the point of view of the child (as a learner) and the adult (as someone who is trying to teach them). This will enable us to think more about the adaptations that you will need to make to promote and facilitate this learning.

Chapter 2

# IMPLICATIONS FOR TEACHING AND LEARNING

In the first chapter we set out to describe PDA and give an overview of some of the research and clinical understandings of the profile. This book, though, is intended for educational practitioners, whose primary concern is the teaching and learning of the pupils that they work with. The rest of the book will have this as its focus and it will start by considering the implications that PDA has both for the pupil and for you. One of the most important things to bear in mind is that every interaction with a child is transactional (or two way) in nature. This means that as well as considering the child's behaviour and response, and the things that contribute to it, you will need to consider your own. This means asking questions of yourself, such as how you might have contributed to a difficult situation (or a successful one!) or what your own reaction was to what the child said or the way that they behaved.

Children with PDA will be catered for in a range of different placements and you may be working with such a pupil in a mainstream school or some type of specialist setting. The pupil may be receiving additional support of one sort or another or might be one of the class group without any extra help. You might be the class teacher, teaching assistant, outreach worker or part of the school leadership team. What will be the case for all of these different settings, and the roles of adults within them, is that adaptations of one sort or another will be needed to meet the needs of a child with the profile of development and behaviour that has been described. These adaptations may be considerable and are likely to be needed both at an organisational level and in terms of personal style.

So what are some of the implications for the pupil and how does it impact on their learning? Let's start by thinking about their point of view and try seeing things from their perspective. This should give us a starting point to think about some of the adaptations that you will need to make to how you plan for a child with PDA and the adjustments you will need to make to the strategies that you use. The first point is to recognise and accept that PDA is best understood as an anxiety-driven need to be in control and avoid other people's demands and expectations. The pupil is often driven by anxieties and uncertainties, which results in them needing to be in control of the choice of activities, the way in which they do things and other people's responses. This means that direction and instruction can be very difficult and they find it hard to compromise or accommodate other people's needs. The fact that they can't find a way to comply with what you are asking of them at any particular point of time is, at that moment, a genuine incapacity. As we have said in other publications, and was first put to us by a parent, 'She can't help won't.'

This understanding and acceptance can be difficult to reach for some people, especially when many children with PDA can be very variable in their mood and behaviour. This can often mean that they are different, to a greater or lesser extent, with different people, in various settings and at different times. This is usually linked to their level of anxiety, which can vary according to all these circumstances and impacts on their tolerance. Linked to this is that the various adults in school may perceive the pupil and the reasons for their behaviour very differently. This is likely to be because they know them less well or see them only at certain times or doing certain activities. These 'glimpses' may not reveal the full picture that someone has who knows them more intimately.

In Chapter 6 we describe an approach which focuses on developing social and emotional understanding, utilising regular sessions referred to as Personal Tutorials. One pupil, talking during a Personal Tutorial, said:

> I am affected by PDA more at home than at school really. I can't control or predict when it's going to happen but I can tell once it is happening to me. It's like I have two messages at the same time; one says, 'Go on, just get in the shower,' but the other blocks it.

It stops me actually moving my legs to get up to have a shower. It holds me back from co-operating. Sometimes I can overcome it but other times it's too strong. It takes a massive effort to overcome it and it's frustrating that other people don't understand how hard that is.

In his video clip Isaac also goes on to talk about this frustration of having 'the functional capacity' to do something but that 'the functional ability isn't there'.

It's the most frustrating thing in the entire universe. So, I know I should be able to get up out of bed and eat properly and drink properly. I know I should be able to make my own food. I should be able to wash every day and change my clothes every day. I know these things... I know how to do them but most of the time I can't... I just can't and without being able to voice why...it's the most frustrating thing.

Explosive behaviour or meltdowns are relatively common in pupils with PDA. Such outbursts can take the form of shouting, screaming, throwing things and lashing out, often in sudden and dramatic ways. Trying to make sense of these episodes from the child's point of view, they are best seen as a panic attack. They usually come on when the pupil can't accommodate to the demands or pressure they feel under and, at that time, can't react in a more adaptive way (by, for example, asking for help or reassurance or explanation). Some of the issues around dealing with this sort of behaviour can be found in the section in Chapter 4 'Managing Meltdowns'.

Isaac also talks about having a panic attack when pressed too directly to do something and that this can come on without a gradual build-up.

If it's direct...if someone is sitting next to me and going 'you have to do this'...it comes straight out as panic, there's no gradual increase. I will immediately start panicking... It goes from 'I'm sort of being OK' to crashing downhill in like three seconds.

While this explosive behaviour is not unusual, there are other children, with different personalities, who are less likely to explode but are adept at 'slipping under the radar'. A high proportion of these children are girls, whose social, communication and behavioural challenges can be masked. You may find that these are the pupils making themselves 'busy' by sharpening the pencils, 'helping' the other children, taking messages and errands or quietly occupying themselves with their own choice of activity. These more subtle forms of avoidance are less obvious and don't present so much of a challenge but can result in the pupil not engaging very much in the intended activity.

The extent of engagement for these pupils who have a lower profile in terms of their behaviour means that frequent monitoring and review of their learning is necessary. This is also the case for all children with PDA over time, ensuring that their learning is embedded and retained. Experience has shown that there can be a real fragility and lack of permanence in their learning. Things can seem to have been understood, learned and demonstrated on one occasion, or over one period of time, but, later, this appears not to have been the case. This might be due to the variability in their anxiety levels, the way they relate to specific people or that their engagement is dependent on a particular form of presentation. Ways that you might help pupils with PDA to understand and manage their anxiety, support them to develop self-reliance and encourage their resilience are discussed further in Chapter 7.

In the main we have focused the discussion about the implications of PDA on the pupil's anxiety, their need to be in control and their avoidance of expectations. We must also remember that pupils with this profile, like others on the autism spectrum, have differences in their social and emotional understanding and their emotional and sensory regulation.

In the first chapter we mentioned that children with PDA can appear sociable on the surface and it is often the case that this misleads people into thinking that they are more capable than is actually the case. In a school setting the pupil is likely to want to interact with other pupils and have friendships more than you would expect of most children on the autism spectrum. Often though the child inadvertently sabotages them by always wanting to be in charge and trying to control others. There can be an 'obsessional' feel to some of these relationships. For example, they may develop a very strong liking and attachment to another pupil and then resent them having contact with others in the class. This might mean that they try to manipulate or referee the other pupil's interactions. They may also blame and victimise other children for things that have gone wrong, even though it is, at least in part, attributable to their own behaviour. For some this can include the holding of grudges.

So far we have talked about the implications that the PDA profile has on a pupil and their capacity to learn. What are the implications for you, as a teacher, and the way in which you set about enabling that learning?

Perhaps the first and most important implication for any adult working with a pupil with PDA is the need to gain as full an understanding as possible about the nature and reasons underpinning their behaviour; both in a general sense about the PDA profile and, more specifically, about the characteristics and behaviours of the individual child. When thinking about a pupil's behaviour we need to understand the why as well as the what. It's not enough to see the behaviour in front of us without trying to gain an understanding about what is underpinning it: why is it happening? To start with, developing this understanding is to do with our attitudes and beliefs as much as it is about our knowledge, skills and expertise. If we understand and hold the view that the pupil's avoidance is an anxiety-driven need to be in control and avoid other people's demands and expectations we realise, using the description we gave earlier in the chapter, that they can't help the fact that they won't do it on this occasion. This doesn't mean that we somehow give up, or give in, in particular situations. It does mean that we realise that the pupil's anxiety is behind the need to avoid at this time. It then follows that it is our responsibility as the adult to come up with ways in which we can help them become less anxious and, as a consequence, more tolerant and enabled to do more of what we expect. Unfortunately, some adults seem to find truly understanding this very difficult. This often leads them down the path of seeing the pupil's avoidance as being wilful and deliberate. Following this belief encourages some people to think that it is their responsibility to impose their choice and decision on the child or young person.

The main reason behind developing specific guidelines for this group of pupils was that overconfrontational, direct and behavioural approaches simply didn't work with children who have a PDA profile. Indeed, more often they resulted in an increase in the pupil's an-xiety and more tension surrounding their relationships. This almost always resulted in the avoidance and behaviour escalating. Throughout subsequent chapters, as we say more about Collaborative Approaches to Learning, we will emphasise the need for a non-confrontational, indirect and adaptive approach. The implication of this for you is to develop that personal teaching style in a creative and flexible way. In order to do this it is important to be reflective in the way that you work and to be open and collaborative with your colleagues. That way you can look back on interactions that have gone well, or not so well, and learn from these for the future. Chapter 9, 'Looking After Yourself', considers some ways to help with this.

One of the questions teachers most frequently ask is 'What about ground rules and boundaries?' While we advocate an indirect and non-confrontational approach we are not saying there are no ground rules, boundaries or 'non-negotiables'. Indeed, staff need to be calm, confident and quietly insistent in maintaining ground rules and boundaries, remembering that there is a difference between being persistent and insistent. In Chapter 4 on strategies we discuss ways in which you might consider priorities for a pupil (which of our expectations are really important at the moment?) and what is helpful in implementing these priorities. Of course, agreed priorities will need to be constantly monitored and reviewed with the intention of progressively increasing these as the pupil becomes more trusting and tolerant. It is likely that on a day-to-day basis expectations will need to be adapted according to the pupil's mood and level of tolerance. In our earlier publication (Christie *et al.* 2012) we used a diagram depicting dials as a way of representing the interplay between the pupil's level of tolerance and what might be expected by the adult. The key challenge to you in teaching and managing a child with PDA is getting the right balance between your expectations and the child's capacity to cope; so it is worth repeating here in Figure 2.1.

It is best to see the pupil as having a particular 'threshold' in relation to his capacity for accepting demands. This threshold will be determined by the level of anxiety that he feels at any given point in time. His level of anxiety can, in turn, be influenced by a multitude of factors which include short-term influences (e.g. how well he slept the night before, whether a trusted member of staff is present or absent, what another child said to him on his way across the playground, etc.) or longer-term ones (e.g. he is in a settled phase with trusting relationships, he has just moved up from primary school, etc.). When things are going well and his anxiety is comparatively low this threshold is higher and he can be more accepting of demands and requests. During a more difficult time, his anxiety is raised and his threshold is lower. At these times he is less tolerant, feels the need to be more controlling and is easily 'tipped over the edge'.

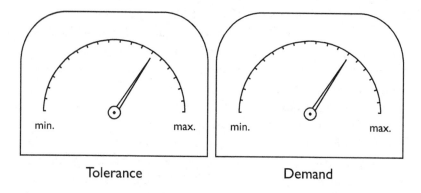

Tolerance              Demand

*Figure 2.1 Synchronising adult's expectations with child's tolerance*

Figure 2.1 shows two dials, one of which gives a measure of the level of the child's threshold or tolerance, the other represents the extent of demand that he experiences. At times, when his threshold is high, it is possible to raise expectations and increase demands. On the other hand, when his threshold is low, the dial showing the level of demand needs to be adjusted to the left, reducing the pressure he feels. The adult has to try to keep the two dials in synchrony for as much time as possible. The frequency with which these dials will need adjusting varies from pupil to pupil and will change over time. There will be spells when the dials need almost constant fine-tuning to try to keep things on as even a keel as possible. In other situations there might be quite long settled spells when much less adjustment is needed. While long settled spells are, of course, encouraging for everybody it is important to guard against complacency. So many teachers and parents report to us how good spells can be punctuated by a sudden 'blip' and describe how they had 'let slide some of the things we had been doing that had enabled him to become more tolerant'.

At the start of the chapter we talked about the need for adaptation, not just at the personal level but also at the organisational level, whichever type of setting the pupil may be attending. One factor that is critical to successful provision for a pupil with a PDA profile is the attitude and approach of the school leadership team. Of course, the amount of adaptation and differentiation that is required by a particular pupil varies according to their need. For many pupils with PDA, though, this will be considerable. Research was carried out at the National Autistic Society's Robert Ogden School by the Centre for Research in Autism and Education (Brede *et al.* 2016). This work followed a group of 'hard-to-include' children with autism, many of whom had a demand avoidant profile, who were reintegrating into school life within the Inclusive Learning Hub at the school. One of the key factors for success was the making of key adjustments to the physical environment, including the provision of individual rooms as a secure base from which to learn to socialise and retreat to when necessary, and using a flexible approach, 'accommodating them on an often moment-by-moment basis' (p.48). Emma Gore Langton and Zoe Syson (n.d.), in a booklet written following up the experiences of nine children with PDA in mainstream settings, also describe the importance of creating space within the classroom or school where a child can go to feel calm. These sort of adjustments often require support beyond the classroom.

If staff working in the classroom need to be flexible and indirect in their approach and personalise the curriculum to a significant extent then this requires understanding and support throughout the school. It might also include flexibility in the time that the pupil arrives at school. The morning routine and getting somewhere at a particular time can be a particular challenge.

During one assessment Oscar's parents described how, at home, mornings and bedtimes are the most stressful times of the day. His mum said, 'It's like he sets off a nuclear bomb, but he is quite calm in the middle of it all. Its like he's pushed all the buttons. You can say "brush your teeth" and he'll have a tantrum and will even run off up the road.' In the mornings he will not get up. She has to dress him in bed. He lies there passively and lets her do it. He will not sit at the table for breakfast, but sits on the floor by the radiator and drinks tea. She may have to make the tea four times as it will not be right for him. He is offered two or three different things for his breakfast but refuses all of them. He then tells his parents that he is hungry at about 8.30am, just as they should be leaving for school, and then eats some cereal or toast.

This was echoed by Ricardo's parents, who reported that the mornings before school were particularly difficult because they were rushing him to get ready and asking him to do things. It would often take two people to dress him and some days he would arrive late, minus his shoes or other items. This was a daily occurrence for most of his previous year at school.

Other children may have had a difficult time in a previous setting and, for a while, arriving after the hurly burly at the start of the school day might be in their interests. The timetable itself may need adjustment in terms of the amount of time spent on particular subjects or where learning takes place; some of this may need to be out of the classroom. Another issue might be the extent of the 'adjustment' to whole school practice or policy that is needed to include a particular pupil, such as the uniform policy, arrangements for assembly or break time and so on. Classroom staff need to feel confident and supported in being able to ensure sufficient differentiation and personalisation both in the curriculum offered and the way in which it is delivered. Sometimes the necessary level of adaptation is comparatively easily managed by the staff within the pupil's class group. It may, though, be less easily accepted and achieved throughout the school as a whole. This may be because there has been insufficient information, they find it hard to understand or accept the level of differentiation required or they are worried about the impact on other pupils in the school. This may cause conflicts and underlines the need for strong leadership, good communication and whole school training.

## Chapter 3

# WHAT ARE COLLABORATIVE APPROACHES TO LEARNING?

Soon after the initial clinical descriptions of PDA were published Elizabeth Newson and those of us working with her were keen to produce some form of guidelines for parents and professionals living and working with children with PDA. These guidelines needed to encapsulate the key features about emphasis and approach that seemed to be most effective for these children, highlighting the differences to those more typically advocated for children on the autism spectrum. The guidelines were written up and published internally in 1998 as *Education and Handling Guidelines for Children with PDA* and quickly became referred to as the 'PDA strategies'. Over time and with experience and feedback these gradually became refined and developed in an article in *Good Autism Practice* (Christie 2007) and then within the first of our Jessica Kingsley publications (Christie *et al.* 2012).

For some time we have tried to find a term, or name, that best captures the approach being advocated that would help make it easier to share this developing methodology with others. This hasn't been an easy task because, in essence, the 'PDA strategies' are about personalisation and flexibility. They are very much about an approach and a style, rather than a set of prescribed methods and strategies that can be consistently applied and adhered to. In the end we felt that the core principle was about collaboration: working with the child or young person, finding a way to negotiate solutions, adjusting expectations, compromising on outcomes and collaborating closely with parents and others. This is not to say that there are no strategies. There are approaches and suggested ideas that work much of the time for many of the children. They do, though, need to be monitored and adapted, reviewed and reconsidered, abandoned for a while and revisited. These strategies will be set out in the next chapters, together with a section on how you might get started adopting this approach in your own setting and situation.

Before this it is important to think about the principles behind these strategies, so that the methods adopted are embedded in an overall framework.

So what are the key principles underpinning Collaborative Approaches to Learning?

## Observe and listen

Everyone working in classroom settings uses all sorts of past experiences (e.g. what has worked well with other children, how they have seen colleagues work, what they have learned from courses and training, the practice and policies within the school, etc.) to develop an approach that they feel comfortable with and put systems in place within the classroom. In the case of those with experience of children with autism these systems are likely to include using a degree of structure, routine and predictability and supporting this with visual systems, such as schedules, timetables and ways of conveying expectations. There may be an element of whole class (or whole school) systems with varying degrees of individual adaptations. Such methodology can be very useful for children with a PDA profile but is likely to require much more in the way of individual adaptation than would be expected for other children. It can be tempting to think that the systems and structures that have been found so helpful in the past, to support other children and the class as a whole, can also be applied to the child with PDA without too much adjustment. For most children with PDA, though, too much structure and routine will come across as overly confrontational, especially when their anxiety levels are high and if they have had difficult experiences at other times when they have been in school. This is especially the case when they are expected to conform to systems that are applied to a whole class or other group too soon. It is critical with a child with such a complex profile to find ways and time to sit back a little, to observe when you can (this might include time in a previous setting, at home, during a preliminary visit, within your own class, etc.), to listen to what other people have said works well and not so well and to hear what the child is able to tell you in any way they are able to. Time spent getting a better understanding of the child and the circumstances that enable their best engagement, and building a rapport with them will not be wasted. It will also allow for a much more personalised approach.

## Work together towards a negotiated solution

It is typically the case that children with PDA will be seen and perceived differently by different people. This is partly due to the complexity of understanding the child's behaviour and the reasons behind it. It may also be because the child seems quite variable in the way that they behave with different people and in different settings. It is also the case that the different adults in their life won't always have the same priorities for the child. There may be different priorities in relation to their behaviour, what is most important for them to learn and what to focus on, both in the short term as well as looking further ahead. The crucial issue of how best to work together to choose priorities is discussed in Chapter 4. The important thing to bear in mind here is that the best solutions are likely to be ones which are negotiated and agreed and that no one person should consider their own views alone without taking others into account. In particular the views of parents and school staff may not be the same; the priorities for home and school life are often different. Some parents of children with a PDA profile may have become distrustful of professionals, often as a result of finding it very hard to agree a diagnostic formulation that helps make sense of their child. Others feel that their parenting skills have been brought into question and that, in some cases, is seen as the reason for the child's behaviour. School staff and parents have to try to find a way of working together to build up a picture of the child as a whole so that they can start planning ahead. This means listening to each other's perspectives and respecting each other's views.

The child's own views also need to be carefully considered and incorporated, both in planning priorities and also in determining what is an 'acceptable' solution or outcome. Of course, many children will find it difficult to articulate these sorts of issues effectively or will find it very hard to see any point of view other than their own. In the long term, working with a child to develop their self-awareness and social understanding that will enable them to become part of these sorts of negotiations becomes an objective, and is referred to in Chapter 7 on promoting social and emotional understanding. In the short term the adults supporting the child will have to take responsibility for trying to see things from the child's point of view and incorporating this into their planning and responses.

## Personalise learning experiences

If we are to maximise the child's level of engagement in learning experiences then we need to be prepared to start with what they are most interested in, even when this may seem to be very narrow and restricted, often based around something that we might describe as a fascination or 'special interest'. With flexibility and imagination it is likely that we can incorporate many different curriculum areas within these interests, or look at how a particular subject area might best be accessed through it. The personalisation is likely to include both the way in which a subject area can be accessed and the content, and further discussion of this, together with examples, takes place in Chapter 6. Of course, the extent of this adaptation will vary from one child to another and any teacher or school will want to ensure that as wide a curriculum as possible can be made accessible to the child. In the early stages, though, in order to build up any rapport or engagement at all, the level of individualisation may need to be very great indeed.

## Modify teaching style: Be flexible, adjust expectations and be less direct

While we have stressed the need for a very individual approach, the essence of the style that has been found to be most effective is one that is non-confrontational, less direct than would usually be the case with other children and very flexible in nature. The whole emphasis needs to be on doing things *with* the child rather than *to* them. Much teaching within schools can feel very instructional and directive in many ways. For the child with PDA this often makes them feel anxious and out of control. This in turn can lead to an increase in their demand avoidance and an escalation of a range of behaviours that can be disruptive to the classroom.

It can be a challenge for teachers to adapt and modify their teaching style to one that is less directive and includes more negotiation and invitation. An example of this difficulty is with the style of language used. Those experienced in working with children with a more typical presentation of autism will be aware of the need for using clear, concise language and reducing ambiguity and redundant information. For a child with a PDA profile, though, this style can often come across as too instructional and confrontational and an indirect suggestion can be easier for the child to process and respond to. Chapter 4 has a section on what can be described as 'using an invitational approach'.

## Flexibility and accommodation

Flexibility may need to take many forms dependent on how much or how little the pupil is able to access learning and participate in school life. For children whose participation is very limited there will need to be a lot of flexibility at an organisational level, as we have mentioned earlier. This might need to include the amount of time the child is in school or in class, the time that they start or finish their school day or whether or not they access certain activities such as assembly or play times. Consideration may need to be given to how whole school policies around, for example, uniform, homework or behaviour are adapted in response to their individual needs and circumstances. It is certainly the case for the more avoidant children that the school leadership team will be integral in supporting the level of accommodation that will be needed for the necessary flexibility in teaching style.

Within the classroom careful thought will need to be given to what is necessary and practical in terms of differentiation. This doesn't just refer to content of the curriculum but the way in which it is delivered.

## Minimise anxiety to maximise learning opportunities

If we understand and accept that anxiety is at the heart of the child's difficulties with co-operating with other people's demands and meeting their expectations then it follows that we need to look at ways that we can reduce that anxiety. Much of this is in the way we modify the teaching approach to be less pressurising and more accommodating. We also need to take account of ways we can reduce that anxiety by considering if we can avoid or moderate certain situations that might cause the child to be anxious in the first place. It might also be helpful to consider introducing or increasing the amount of time that the child has access to activities that they find calming and regulating. Of course these will be different for each individual but might include relaxation techniques, mindfulness, physical activity or quiet periods of engagement based on a favoured interest.

## Monitor, reflect and review

Especially when we are planning ways to respond to more challenging aspects of behaviour it can be tempting to meet, plan a programme of intervention and agree a time period during which everyone involved consistently applies what has been agreed. As we have already outlined, for children with a PDA profile there is a need to be much more flexible and make adjustments according to the situation and their level of anxiety. There is, though, a need for all involved to monitor what has worked well or not so well, reflect on why this might be and use that to inform our future responses. In Chapter 9 there is a useful checklist of questions which can be helpful to frame this reflection and discussion. Comments from parents and teachers often include remarks like 'nothing works for long'. That may be the case but it doesn't mean that you can't come back to it in the future and find it effective once more.

## Be proactive: Foster emotional resilience, independence and self-reliance

Much of what we outline as strategies are in one sense short term. They attempt to look at ways that we can modify the environment, organisation and the way people relate to the child. This is aimed at reducing the child's level of anxiety, helping them feel less pressurised and in turn more amenable to the suggestions and expectations that people have of them. Improving this can make an enormous difference to children who have become extremely stressed and reluctant to engage. We hope, too, that this has a cumulative effect and that as the child participates more they become less anxious and more trusting with a wider range of people and in more situations. We need to be aware, though, that gains made can be fragile and tenuous and dependent on certain individuals and the adoption of specific approaches. Take these away and there are times when the levels of anxiety and disruptive behaviour increase again. We don't want to diminish the value of getting the modifications right and without this there can often be no place to start. At the same time, though, we need to keep one eye on the future and think about ways in which we might enable the young person themselves to become more self-aware, and better able to communicate their anxieties in an effective way and manage and regulate their own emotions. Chapter 7 looks at this in much more detail.

## Recognise the needs of adults

As well as having their own perspectives on a child, as we described earlier, different adults have different needs in respect of their circumstances and relationships with the child. The particular needs and pressures on family members are well described by Margot Duncan in *Understanding Pathological Demand Avoidance in Children* (Christie *et al.* 2012). This current book, though, has as its focus those adults working in education settings. The needs of staff are often given insufficient attention in schools. Teaching and learning is a transactional (two-way) process and while, inevitably, the focus is on the needs of the child it is also important to recognise and understand those of the adults who support them. As part of the leadership of a specialist provision for children with autism this was very high on our agenda. If we are going to best support the needs of the child it is critical to understand the pressures on staff and support them in terms of their professional development, capacity to problem-solve, teamwork and resilience. Some ways of ensuring these areas are developed are discussed more fully in Chapter 9.

Chapter 4

# KEY STRATEGIES

This chapter will provide you with some key strategies. You may be able to use some of these ideas very quickly and effectively with the pupils you support. Others may need adaptation or may not be quite the 'right fit' for the child you know at the moment. This doesn't mean they will not be worth revisiting in the future.

You are going to need a range of strategies for pupils with PDA in order to keep their engagement and interest. You will also need to develop strategies that work on their most difficult days as well as their best days.

The strategies in this section build on your understanding of the principles of Collaborative Approaches to Learning set out in Chapter 3 and include:

- **Choose priorities**: What is important now and what can we come back to later?

- **Putting priorities into place**: How can we deal with what we've decided is important? What is helpful to keep in mind about implementing priorities?

- **Use an invitational approach**: How can we increase the likelihood of co-operation by enabling a child to join us?

- **Think out loud**: Sharing our thinking process with a child to model problem-solving and to encourage them to participate.

- **Be indirect**: How can we present this request without being directive?

- **Make accommodations**: What adjustments can we make to maximise participation?

- **Use socially complex language**: How can being conversational seem more indirect?

- **Use routines**: How can we adapt routines to help?

- **Adapt visual strategies**: What different emphasis do we need to use visual strategies successfully?

- **Provide extra processing time**: How can we build in more processing time and what are the advantages of doing so?

- **Use drama and role play**: How can drama be helpful?

- **Use novelty and variety**: How can we use surprises to engage a child with PDA?

- **Avoid unnecessary confrontation**: What do we need to consider when it looks like there could be a confrontation? How can we adjust expectations and use distraction and planned ignoring? How can we legitimise behaviour and employ choices and alternatives?

- **Manage meltdowns**: How can we manage a meltdown to promote good outcomes for everyone?

- **Promote self-awareness and emotional wellbeing**: How can we protect and promote social and emotional wellbeing?

- **Personalise the curriculum**: How can we individualise learning opportunities and priorities?

- **Adjust the use of rewards and sanctions**: How should we respond when things go well and when they don't?

 ## Choose priorities

Although there are lots of issues that may be priorities for the school, the family and the young person themselves it is important to identify a realistic number to work on at a time. It can be helpful to do this using a priority rating chart. This helps take account of everyone's views on how and why decisions are made. It also provides a means of logging issues that you have decided are not high priorities at the moment. You can come back to them later. Table 4.1 is a priority rating chart for the settling-in period for a 9-year-old girl who had been out of school for a year and was transitioning into her new mainstream placement. The column on the left lists priorities that the team had raised. The column in the middle shows whether the issue was judged to be a high, medium or low priority. The column on the right offers a rationale for the priority and comments about the responses of the adults.

**Table 4.1 Priority rating chart example 1**

| Lucy Class 4, age 9.3 yrs | | |
|---|---|---|
| How important is it that she… | Priority level | Comments, rationale and plan |
| Feels positive about coming to school | High | Key staff will prioritise building relationships with Lucy and offer project work based around her interests. Mum and Dad will provide a list of current favourites and will not use these resources at home so that coming to school is more motivating for her. |
| Does not hurt herself or others | High | This is non-negotiable. It will be explained to Lucy that staff will intervene should this happen and that it will be discussed with her parents. |
| Does not seriously damage school property | High | This is non-negotiable, therefore staff will need agreement regarding what is considered serious damage, e.g. deliberately snapping pencils is not serious (it is probably an indicator of stress which should prompt staff to respond to reduce anxiety) whereas kicking cupboard doors off their hinges would be viewed as serious damage. |
| Participates in daily activities which have been identified to regulate her, e.g. looking after the guinea pig | High | Lucy has low self-esteem and high anxiety which can affect her in variable ways from one day to another. She will be offered daily access to activities that regulate her arousal and sensory needs. She will have opportunities to learn through her interests and to complete tasks that build on her successes. She will have 'responsibilities' at school that she can choose, related to looking after the school pets. |
| Wears school uniform | Medium | School uniform colours will be required. Fabrics and style of garment can be her choice, e.g. grey joggers and white polo rather than school trousers and white shirt. |

*cont.*

| How important is it that she... | Priority level | Comments, rationale and plan |
|---|---|---|
| Arrives at school at the same time as the other pupils | Low | Lucy's arrival slot will be between 8:50 and 9:30. No comment will be made or attention drawn to differing arrival times. Staff will work closely with Lucy's mum to support on more difficult days. The hope is that she will choose to arrive alongside other pupils if there is no pressure on her to do so. |
| Attends school daily | High | It is a high priority that Lucy has an educational experience on site which moves her towards full time attendance. It is OK that some days she does her work in the quiet room or on the allotment. An amended and flexible timetable will be available to offer her motivating and regulating activities as necessary. Staying on site is non-negotiable and it will be explained that, should she try to abscond, staff will intervene. She will have a phased entry to school, meaning she starts on part days and builds up time but the intention is that she comes to school at some point every day. |
| Brings own pencil case and maths set (this is a rule in class) | Low | No expectation of this. Equipment to be subtly provided without comment. |
| Stays seated throughout lessons (this is a general class expectation) | Medium | Regular movement breaks will be put in place during lessons to give her valid reasons to leave her seat. These will be gauged by her support staff who can respond flexibly to her needs. |
| Engages in positive social interaction for 15–20-minute slots with adults and other pupils | High | Support staff will have additional time set aside to interact and to get to know her through her interests and projects. Time will be facilitated with a small group of other pupils to play together with adult guidance as necessary and for short but positive time slots. |
| Completed in consultation with: Lucy's mum and dad Class teacher Special educational needs co-ordinator (SENCO) Teaching assistant Home support tutor | Date | Next review of the above planned for: |

There is a blank downloadable priority rating chart in the Appendix.

Table 4.1 focuses on some of the broader aspects of attending school. You may also write charts with a focus on specific areas such as engagement in taught activities, such as shown in Table 4.2.

Table 4.2 Priority rating chart example 2

| Lucy<br>Class 4, age 9.3 yrs | | |
|---|---|---|
| How important is it that she... | Priority level | Comments and rationale |
| Completes her classroom work in writing | Low | It is important that Lucy engages in work tasks but recording them can be done flexibly. This might mean using photos or iPad, or dictating her words to a scribe who should record verbatim, without 'correcting', so as to capture her own thinking. |
| Has opportunities to complete work tasks through her interest in ponies | High | Lucy benefits from the self-esteem associated with using her area of specialist knowledge. Basing her work around ponies is soothing as well as motivating for her. Staff to use their creative teaching skills to adapt her work while also keeping in mind the options for extending her interests or including her in other classroom activities if they appeal to her. |
| Completes a required set of tasks each day | High | There are a number of required slots in her daily timetable but Lucy has control over the order in which she does them. |
| Works in the classroom | Medium | It is important that Lucy is not overloaded. If the focus of the work is on more complex academic learning or if her mood is delicate then this is best done in the quieter learning zone. If the learning focus is on social interaction or is on a less challenging curriculum area for her then doing it in the classroom is to be encouraged. |
| Completed in consultation with:<br><br>Lucy's mum and dad<br>Class teacher<br>SENCO<br>Teaching assistant | Date | Review of the above planned for: |

## Putting the priorities into place

First, all the adults involved need to be clear about the priorities identified and why these have been chosen. They need to understand and agree the rationale behind the decisions. This will enable the adults to uphold the high priorities, support each other and use their initiative to be flexible about the medium and low priorities.

Second, there needs to be a co-ordinated plan for how school staff will respond if a high priority is challenged. The plan needs to be set out in the strategies and will hopefully prevent challenges in the first place. However, you will need an agreed and co-ordinated response if it should become necessary. In this respect there are a few basic recommendations:

- **Stay calm yourself:** Certainly do your best to come across as calm even if you don't feel it. Think about the messages you are sending out with your body language; reflect on the tone of voice you are using and the language you choose; notice whether there are any aspects of the immediate environment that are contributing to increased stress which could be improved.

- **Assess the risks** in the environment and the situation. Consider the potential and likely outcomes of both doing and not doing whatever you are considering.

- **Think about the options** that are available to you. Try to remember to offer additional processing time, visual support if appropriate, suggest alternatives or offer distractions that might alter the mood.

- **Communicate** with the other adults so that you respond in a co-ordinated way. Think about where is the best place to be, who are the key people you want to be involved in this situation, when is the wisest moment to intervene?

- **If safety is challenged** and you need to use physical intervention do so with consultation, supervision, parental consent, appropriate training, necessary safeguards, appropriate record keeping and debrief opportunities after the incident.

- **Recovery time and space** for the individuals involved is important, including making time to repair the relationship with the child.

## What is helpful to keep in mind about implementing priorities?

It is not possible to run a school, classroom or family without some boundaries. We need to choose the non-negotiables wisely and be prepared to implement them. As long as confrontation is kept to a minimum, there are positive benefits in upholding carefully chosen priorities:

- Boundaries that are reasonable and are chosen to keep everyone safe are reassuring.

- Demonstrating to a child with PDA that we are committed to upholding the agreed priorities, including those that they view as important to them, can strengthen our relationship with them.

- It is easier for school staff to work in a calm and cohesive way if they are supported by agreed boundaries.

- Realistic priorities can set out a route to success and achievements for the child which will leave everyone feeling encouraged.

 ## Use an invitational approach

Although there are a number of strategies set out within Collaborative Approaches to Learning, this is the one that really gets to the heart of the approach. It characterises the tone and style of our most successful interactions with pupils with PDA. It should be our benchmark for testing how well we are facilitating participation.

Children with PDA often respond well to an approach that encourages them to join in, rather than one which directs or requires them to do so. This is not how school staff generally present activities to pupils so doing this fluently will take some practice. As you get more accustomed to using an invitational approach it will start to feel more natural. It becomes easier to find an element of most requests that offer invitational choice. Even if the core point is less flexible look for an opportunity for choice that doesn't matter to the task in hand. For instance:

'Do you want to use crayons or felt tips to do this worksheet?'

'Should I read Horrid Henry's joke book or the Guinness Book of Records while we are waiting for dinner?'

The strengths of an invitational approach are that it can be tailored to appeal to a child's interests or their sense of humour, and giving children with PDA additional control in a negotiation will reduce their anxiety, which in itself will result in a higher chance of co-operation.

Invitational approaches particularly appeal to children who are sometimes described as feeling as though they have similar rights to adults. Most adults respond best when they are given choices and are asked politely and respectfully to contribute to a work task.

One 19-year-old pupil attending an ASC specialist day school described:

> If a direct request is part of a normal conversation, it's easier for me to co-operate with. If it feels a gentle question mixed in with a friendly chat it is much easier than having an instruction.

Getting this balance right for a pupil with PDA can be done by simply adjusting our language, such as:

'When you have a minute I wondered whether you might…'

'Please would you be able to help me with…'

'If only there was someone who could help me figure this out…'

'It would be great if this could get done today. I'd love to help you with it. Should we do it in the hall or the library?'

'Let's talk about last night's football match while we walk to the classroom where X is ready. What did you think of that penalty?'

 **Think out loud**

Another way of being incidental and invitational is for an adult to start the activity while thinking out loud, posing rhetorical questions, making deliberate mistakes or appealing to the child's sense of humour. It might capture the child's attention if an activity can be based on an area of interest or strength. If you can match the task to a child's genuine skill or subject in which they have some expertise it will improve their self-esteem as well as their participation.

It is important that even once the child has begun to engage with an activity we continue to offer this flexible and indirect style. It should characterise how we interact with them as much of the time as we can manage. It should not be the way we draw a child into a task, then reverting to giving instructions. Maintaining this style will also help us to use invitational approaches more naturally and authentically.

Making deliberate errors is most effective for younger children but can be adapted for older pupils. The themes to characterise your approach need to be inviting, respectful and fun. For example, you might encourage a young child to complete a number inset puzzle by making deliberate mistakes and hoping that they will correct you. You might present a similar task to an older child (who will be well aware that you do actually know your numbers) by setting yourself the challenge of trying to complete the task with your eyes closed. In this way you can create a fun interactive game. You can give them the role of invigilator to check you don't cheat and they can grade your performance, which is how you can determine their knowledge.

Thinking out loud is also an effective and indirect way of modelling self-talk and problem-solving skills. These are likely to be key areas of learning for a child with PDA, who may be unaware of how other people process all sorts of information.

It may include dropping comments that are task related, such as:

'I'm wondering what will happen if I take another brick out of this Jenga. I think it could all collapse so I can't quite decide whether to do it…'

Or it could be related to modelling social problem-solving such as in conversation with a pupil, saying:

'I could tell that your friend Alex was a bit upset this morning because he was quiet. He said he was sad about after school club being cancelled. I'm going to ask him to do some goal practice with me at lunchtime to see if that cheers him up. I like playing football with him anyway…'

Or could be about a specific learning task, such as:

> 'I've heated water in the test tube. What does that say to add next? Ah, the acid compound. I wonder what will happen now…let me see…'

##  Be indirect

A delicate balance of structure and indirectness works well with pupils with PDA. A degree of structure that reassures them about what their day will bring is useful because it reduces anxiety. How that structure is presented needs to be flexible so as not to seem too directive. If it builds on the child's confidence and on the relationship between the adult and the child it will promote more positive interactions in the future too.

Sometimes being indirect may be as straightforward as leaving teaching materials on a table without drawing the child's attention to them. This could be done in a very low-key way. Alternatively it may work well to include an element of the third person, such as:

> 'Who's left this here? What is it anyway?'

Or some script that offers the child choice and a position of being in charge, such as:

> 'Oh, that activity looks too tricky for me. I could only do it if someone clever was there to help me. I think we should put it away. What do you think?'

This strategy will *allow the child to take the lead* in the activity and to engage with it. In this example, they might also agree with you and choose to put it away so you would need to be open to either outcome.

It can be beneficial to be aware of a less direct approach to how we *give pupils personal space*. For instance, it might be better to sit next to or even slightly behind a child rather than facing them. It might be better to imply they sit down by moving a chair towards them rather than specifically asking or telling them to do so.

You can be indirect by *depersonalising the expectation*. Rather than it being *your* request it might be what the worksheet asks for, or what the government needs schools to do. It might be a legal obligation that schools provide such and such. It might be a requirement of health and safety policies. This third-party 'voice' can be a way to recognise the child's frustration at the request while you nonetheless adhere to it.

Some children respond well to being given a responsibility, such as being put 'in charge of' a certain job within the school. There may be designated slots of the school day or week when they can participate better in the guise of this role. A responsibility can give children opportunities to develop independence, problem-solving skills and social interaction. School settings which have found this useful have created responsibilities for pupils such as fruit and snack distribution, setting up equipment for PE or assembly, managing inventories for playground equipment, ordering books for the school library and so on.

Examples of what being indirect might look like are shown in Tables 4.3 and 4.4. A downloadable chart is available in the Appendix.

**Table 4.3 Adaptation to task example 1**

| Task as planned by class teacher for the group | Task adapted for Martha |
|---|---|
| Make a cake to sell at a charity cake sale.<br><br>Find a recipe for making one cake to sell. | Mrs Milner to support Martha.<br><br>A selection of recipe books to be left out on the work table. Various charity merchandise and toys available. iPad available. |
| Write out the chosen recipe in workbook.<br><br>Write a shopping list for cake ingredients (shopping for the class to be ordered through the school kitchen supplier).<br><br>Design a poster to advertise the charity cake sale. | Mrs Milner to browse recipe books and 'think out loud' about which may be interesting to make or delicious to eat. Mrs Milner to make a shortlist of five cakes they agree look good. Martha will choose one cake that they will make.<br><br>Mrs Milner will write a shopping list (unless Martha prefers to do so).<br><br>Mrs Milner to accompany Martha to the local shop next lesson to buy her ingredients.<br><br>A poster to be created either using paper and art materials or by using the iPad, and taking photos of Martha/Mrs Milner wearing the charity merchandise. |

Table 4.4 Adaptation to task example 2

| Task as planned by class teacher for the group | Task adapted for Adam |
|---|---|
| Science experiment.<br><br>Viscosity testing to be carried out on the following substances: water, milkshake, vegetable oil, glycerine, syrup, PVA glue, salad cream, ketchup.<br><br>Write out the method and equipment required. | Adam to work with a peer supported by Mrs White.<br><br>An equipment list to be available for Adam to tick off when he or his peer has collected what is needed from around the lab.<br><br>Adam to choose whether he wants to take the role of timing each test, recording findings or handling the materials required. |
| Explain what the variables are and how you will make this a fair test.<br><br>Worksheet to be filled out with hypothesis, predictions and findings. | Mrs White to have prepared a personalised worksheet setting out a number of true or false statements.<br><br>Mrs White to make some deliberate errors to determine Adam's understanding of a fair test. |
| Write a sentence summarising your conclusion. | Findings and summary to be discussed and recorded by any one of the group. |

 ## Make accommodations

Children with PDA respond well to flexible approaches. The more options we can keep open to ourselves as well as to the pupil, the more likely we are to achieve co-operation.

For example, it might be difficult for the child to complete a numeracy task of estimating distance between two points and then measuring accurately to confirm the result. This might be because there are other pressures and distractions in a busy classroom or might reflect the challenge and demands of the task itself. The child with PDA may be reluctant to estimate because of the associated risk of getting the answer 'wrong'. Adjusting the task as in Table 4.5 could make all the difference.

Table 4.5 Adapatation to task example 3

| Task as planned by class teacher for the group | Task adapted for Billy |
|---|---|
| Estimate the distance between two points of varying lengths for three items.<br><br>E.g. the length of a side of A4 in mm, the height of the desk in cm, the width of the classroom in metres.<br><br>Complete the table in maths workbook to record work. | Mrs Khan will have three attempts at estimating the distances between each item. Billy will advise her to choose one of those as her final estimate.<br><br>Billy will then test the accuracy of her estimates by measuring and scoring her guesses.<br><br>Mrs Khan will fill in the worksheet unless Billy prefers to.<br><br>For each answer that is +/-15 Billy and Mrs Khan will get an extra five minutes to play chess at the end of the lesson. |

## Use socially complex language

We tend to use clear and concise language with other pupils with autism spectrum conditions. This is because of what we understand about their language and processing strengths and difficulties. The issue with using clear and direct language with children with PDA is that it can feel too instructional. Therefore it's often better to be more conversational, even though this means you will be using more complex language.

To give an everyday classroom example, it would not be unusual to say to a child who has a typical presentation of autism:

'Tom, drawing has finished… Time to put the pens away… Come to stand by the door… We are going to walk to the hall for assembly.'

These instructions may also be supported by signs or symbols.

We might be more successful if we say to a pupil with PDA:

'I can see the others are starting to clear up. It must be nearly time for assembly. I can help you tidy up if you like. Do you want to put your drawing pens away in your tray or are you going to leave them on your desk?… By the way did you notice that bird's nest that Mrs Norris found? It's on the table outside the hall. We can look at it on the way to assembly. I was thinking of putting this chocolate egg in it to give her a surprise! What do you reckon?'

You may be more successful using this less direct approach that includes invitational asking, appeals to personal interests and humour. It contains the same basic requirements of the child, that is, stop drawing and walk to the hall in time for assembly, but does so in an indirect way.

 **Use routines**

There is an element of expectation in everyday routines. For example, sitting at the classroom desk usually indicates that you will soon be asked to do some work. Children with PDA may be finely tuned to these expectations, which may even get in the way of them getting to school in the first place. Some children use anticipating routines to their advantage to avoid demands, such as hiding their PE kit so they can't do sport. However, there can also be benefits of routines. The advantages of routines include:

- They provide a degree of predictability which, if the child can tolerate it and not use it strategically, has the benefit of lowering anxiety.

- The child can input their own detail into an overall structure to give them control and choice within an activity.

- Sometimes children are comfortable getting 'swept along' with the flow of the moment to move them to the next activity.

For Theo it has been identified that getting him into class and settled is a priority. That requires a degree of detailed planning to support him being successful. It might look like Table 4.6.

Table 4.6 Adaptation to routine

| Theo | Class: Blue |
|------|-------------|
| Routine as planned by class teacher for the group | Routine adapted for Theo |
| Children to line up outside then file into the classroom through the main door, hang up their coats and put their school bags away before sitting at their designated desks. | Theo to be greeted outside and given a choice of position in the line (choice of two places). Theo's coat and bag to be put away by teaching assistant (TA) (unless Theo prefers to do it himself). Theo to enter the classroom and be given the choice of sitting at a shared desk or at his work station (motivating activity to be available in both areas). |

**Adapt visual strategies**

Visual strategies are helpful to lots of children on the autism spectrum. This reflects what we know about them, helping to give concrete information that can be processed more definitely and more slowly. Commonly used approaches include schedules and visual systems. These strategies can benefit children with PDA *if the emphasis is adapted to ensure they remain flexible and indirect* rather than being a prescribed to-do list.

For example, a visual timetable for a pupil with autism may look like Table 4.7.

**Table 4.7 Structured visual schedule**

| Today is Wednesday 28 September | Subject | Work task | Tick here when completed |
|---|---|---|---|
| Lesson 1 | English | Complete punctuation sheet, then plan creative writing about The Train Journey | |
| Break | | My class is on the upper playground today | |
| Lesson 2 | Maths | Using Unifix to show my working out and complete the number bonds activity on page 16 in workbook 3a | |
| Lunch | | Lunchtime club today is chess | |
| Lesson 3 | Science | Complete the experiment following the instructions on the worksheet. Stick the worksheet into my science book and write up the results on the opposite page | |
| Home time | | Today take home:<br>• PE kit<br>• letter about the school trip<br>• reading book | |

Similar content can still be presented visually but in a flexible way that is better suited to a pupil with PDA, as in Table 4.8. A downloadable chart is available in the Appendix.

Table 4.8 Flexible visual schedule

| Today is Wednesday 28 September<br><br>These are the choices today<br><br>Mrs Singh will be in class to help you today<br><br>Please decide a timetable together with Mrs Singh | | |
|---|---|---|
| **English** | **Maths** | **Science** |
| Plan a creative story about The Train Journey (this can be written or drawn or Mrs Singh can write it down)<br><br>OR<br><br>Continue working on my personal project folder | Set some number bond tasks up to 20 for Mrs Singh to complete. She can use Unifix and I can help her if she gets stuck with the working out. I can mark her work<br><br>OR<br><br>Make a tessellation pattern to cover my personal project folder. I can choose any card or wrapping paper from the Art cupboard | Choose at least 4 of the 8 objects on the table and test them to see if they float or sink. See if Mrs Singh can guess right before she finds out the results.<br><br>Put the results in my science book either by<br><br>• Mrs Singh writing them<br><br>• sticking in a photo<br><br>• writing it myself |
| **Breaktime:**<br><br>Choose:<br><br>Play on the upper playground with my class<br><br>OR<br><br>Go to the library | **Lunchtime activities:**<br><br>Choose:<br><br>• Chess club<br><br>• Play on the field<br><br>• Go to the library | **Home time jobs:**<br><br>Choose one job for me and one job for Mum:<br><br>• Carry my PE kit home<br><br>• Carry my book bag home |

There is quite a lot of written information on these schedules. This can obviously be adapted as necessary. Meaningful and motivating symbols or pictures may also be added.

Visual timetables appeal more to some children with PDA than others but even if a child may be sensitive to certain forms of structured approaches this does not mean that they should be avoided but should be adapted.

An 11-year-old pupil with PDA was in a small class in a special school with other pupils with autism. Each pupil had a daily individual visual timetable displayed on the classroom wall. The purpose of these timetables was to demonstrate to the pupils what was happening that day and the other pupils referred back to their timetable on a number of occasions during the school day. The pupil with PDA was very resistant to having his displayed and repeatedly pulled it down. Following a repeated pattern of the teacher replacing it and the child binning it, his teacher explained to him that, although the timetable had his name on it, it was not actually for him to look at. She told him that it was her responsibility to know what each of the pupils was doing every day because she was accountable if senior management or inspectors came in. She would happily change the name to a nickname so only people who knew him would know it was about him. She said she didn't need or want him to look at it. As the teacher and pupil had a good relationship and he didn't want her to be 'in trouble' he accepted this rationale.

Not surprisingly, over time she noticed him checking his timetable. The teacher didn't refer to him looking at it unless he asked a specific question about it. The teacher kept in mind that the purpose of the timetable was to add clarity and reassurance for the pupil with PDA. It was not necessary to point out that he had been seen using it. She hoped he would become more relaxed about it if there was no pressure on him, which did happen over time.

### Write letters, notes and messages

Children often enjoy receiving letters that are personalised. 'Letters' can arrive in many formats, including electronic variations, though there are advantages in having one saved to a screen or printed out so as to have something tangible to refer to. For some children with PDA letters are not only less directive and give more processing time but can also feel a respectful, adult way to communicate.

A letter might be a useful way to 'invite' a child to an event as well as to set out alternatives if they turn down the initial invitation. It can be a depersonalised way to encourage them to attend or to contribute to a meeting such as their annual review or an appointment. Similarly, letters can be used to summarise what was discussed or agreed in a conversation or meeting.

Letter writing was particularly helpful in supporting a 10-year-old pupil attending a mainstream school whose family wrote:

> It has been a tough time for us. He has been shouting, swearing, hitting his dad and threatening his sister. He thinks he needs to know every conversation between adults. He shouts that he has a right to know and gets frustrated when I tell him it's not about him or it's a conversation for us adults to have... Since school started writing him letters, to which he dictates replies, he has been much calmer. The letters have not really told him more information than we were giving him verbally but he has felt much more included. He has made an elaborate filing system that he keeps up to date and proudly takes a folder to the meetings and appointments he attends.

Written notes, whether on paper or a device, can be a useful and less direct way of communicating with a pupil with PDA. For instance, passing notes back and forth to a child who has retreated to their den/tent in order to re-engage them in communication can be a successful strategy.

> One teenage pupil with PDA was much more forthcoming during discussions about emotional or social issues if he typed a sentence to his key worker in English, then used a translate app to speak it out loud in a language neither of them knew before his key worker typed her reply and did the same. The foreign language element was fun and indirect. The actual conversation about the issue was carried out on screen.

 **Provide extra processing time**

Schools are very busy environments and things change quickly during the school day from one lesson to the next and from one social context to the next. This can be especially difficult for pupils in mainstream secondary settings who, because of their age, are being expected to navigate these situations more independently.

Pupils with PDA need time to process the social, emotional, sensory and curriculum information they are presented with. They also need time to process whether they can tolerate co-operating with a request or expectation at this particular moment.

You can build in time and space for pupils with PDA by:

- considering their work area: you might want them to have access to a calmer, quieter area as well as to the ordinary classroom environment

- offering them tasks or responsibilities that give them regular movement breaks or opportunities to leave the class for an errand

- including the capacity in their daily timetable for time to gather themselves or to recover from sessions that are more challenging or overloading for them; this may not only be in relation to their least favourite lessons but also break and lunchtimes, arrival at school and preparation for the transition home

- including opportunities for regulation which might include sensory activities or relaxing time with a special interest

- thinking about moving around school such as lining up, lunch queues and changing classroom in between lessons, and allowing for more flexible time slots to complete these tasks.

The additional benefit of giving children with PDA extra processing time is that you, as the adult supporting them, also have that time. This can make an important difference to how you feel yourself as well as the way you problem-solve. Sometimes we need more time in order to think creatively, to 'pull a rabbit out of the hat', to distract or re-engage the child we are working with. Other times we may need additional time to calm ourselves and gather our own thoughts if we have been involved in an incident or are starting to feel outmanoeuvered. Recalibrating our own mood and planning ahead takes time. As you give the child processing time try to make sure that you use this same time effectively yourself too.

You will have read in Chapter 2 that an essential technique when you are supporting a child with PDA is to keep the dials of your demand and their tolerance synchronised. Doing this well takes practice but it also requires time to think and reflect.

**Use drama and role play**

Children with PDA are often comfortable in drama and role play. This tends to be particularly true of girls with this profile. Using drama is not only a good way to appeal to the interests of children but is another way of being indirect. When we engage in role play a 'safety buffer' is created between our real selves and our pretend character. For some children with PDA this provides them with the indirectness that suits them. One teacher commented:

> Andy is able to complete most of his work through his hand puppet 'Sandy the Squirrel'. He uses Sandy to do all of his written work. Not surprisingly his handwriting is not as good as it could be because he is using Sandy as a glove but he is at last doing some written work! He swings between putting Sandy down for not being very clever, to praising Sandy very highly because other squirrels can't write at all, let alone messily. We have had a great deal more success with co-operation and therefore with learning since Sandy came to class.

Another example is using the characterisation of a celebrity chef as a successful way of getting a pupil involved not only in a cooking session but also in the associated shopping, planning and reviewing of their food.

Using pretend play may be a good way to earn the trust of a child. They may be more willing to interact with you 'in role'. That means they can get a sense of whether they feel sufficiently comfortable with you to allow you closer.

> As part of her transition to Year 3 in a separate part of the school Zara's new teacher came to visit her in her current class. On the first visit of the unfamiliar teacher Zara was understandably nervous and suspicious of what this person may ask her to do. The teacher introduced herself as Miss Judd. Zara was very polite and introduced herself as 'Maureen' who was Head of Security at the school. She said she needed to take the new teacher through some checks before she could see if Zara was available. There followed a few minutes of airport-style security procedures. Miss

Judd co-operated fully with this and interacted with 'Maureen' throughout. Miss Judd was then shown to the waiting area. 'Maureen' left the room saying she would find out if Zara was free yet. A few minutes later she returned with armfuls of dolls and dressing-up clothes to invite Miss Judd to play with her as Zara.

Miss Judd couldn't have predicted the precise scenario she would find herself in but did very well to respond positively to the situation. Zara had time to gauge Miss Judd while she was interacting as 'Maureen'. Having felt comfortable enough to engage with her she was able to identify an activity they could enjoy together.

You might be able to use drama as a motivating tool to promote engagement with other learning that requires some imagination, such as in subjects like literacy or history as in Table 4.9.

Table 4.9 Adaptation to task example 4

| Task as planned by class teacher for the group | Task adapted for Freya |
| --- | --- |
| Rewrite an alternative scene for the second act of the play we have been studying that could have happened if the Queen had not killed her brother. | Freya to have time in the drama studio with Mr Giles. A range of costumes and props available.<br><br>The scene is set. Freya to choose whether she plays the Queen or her brother. As the alternative scene is acted out with Freya directing, the script is recorded by Mr Giles.<br><br>Freya has final edit of the script. |

Although going along with a child's chosen role can work well, it is also important to ensure they remain in touch with their real self. There are times when children with PDA can blur the lines between reality and fantasy, which obviously has negative implications for their sense of self and their wellbeing. Including regular time for them to connect with their genuine selves, plus adults being careful not to overuse the pretend persona, even if that persona is compliant, is important.

##  Use novelty and variety

Unlike children with a more straightforward presentation of autism, children with PDA can respond well to new and different experiences. Although a certain amount of routine and predictability lowers anxiety which is a good thing, too much can start to feel confining to pupils with PDA. Some may even use the expectations of a routine strategically to block the demand or to shift the goalposts.

As the adults who support these children, we need to find a balance between providing enough variety to be interesting while not presenting them with so much unpredictability that we raise their anxiety. Generally speaking, when we are using a new activity or a surprise it will work best if this is an 'upgrade' or if it involves one of their personal interests. It can be a particularly helpful way of reframing an activity if you need to hastily adjust what you had planned.

Some suggestions of how to introduce variety when you are readjusting the activity include:

> 'Oh dear, I forgot to bring the compass and protractor set. I hope you don't mind if we don't do this maths work just now. We can come back to it tomorrow. I did notice that the art supplies order has arrived. Should we go and see if there's anything you might like to put to one side for your sculpture project?'

> 'Mr Dawlish has sent us this note. It's asking whether someone in our class wants to organise the younger pupils to move the PE equipment to the new shed this afternoon. What do you reckon?'

> 'I've got some carrots for the school guinea pig if you've got time to come with me to feed her. I was also thinking about whether we should use some of this tinsel to decorate her hutch. Do you think she would even notice?'

Using novelty and variety is not about suddenly abandoning learning, it is about presenting a particular teaching point in a range of different ways.

As part of the personalised learning opportunities that you offer pupils with PDA some of their work might be framed within a project. These may be based on their hobbies or strengths. Alternatively, their interest may be captured by setting them a mission or challenge which they are motivated to solve or investigate. These missions or projects are effective because they are not only indirect and individualised ways of presenting learning but they also provide variety. If you establish ongoing or open-ended projects they can be used flexibly. You might, for instance, have a slot on a timetable called 'project time' within which the child has choice over which particular project they work on and which task they do now.

## Avoid unnecessary confrontation

As described in Chapter 3 a key principle of Collaborative Approaches to Learning is to observe and listen. This refers to collaborating with other adults who know the child, as well as the child themselves. It also means that we need to take care to 'tune in' to how the child is responding and therefore how they are feeling at any given time. Doing so will help us to avoid potential flashpoints. Alongside being clear about which issues we are holding as high priorities, and using a flexible interactive style, we will be in a better position to minimise confrontation if we keep an eye on the pupil's mood and engagement.

Children with PDA tend to meet like with like. If we present them with a non-negotiable they are likely to meet us with a non-negotiable. This is why we need to use the analogy of the dials as found in Chapter 2, to keep ourselves adaptable and have options open for the child and the adult.

Tools like the priority rating chart can help us to develop a co-ordinated response to high priority behaviours. Upholding high priorities is discussed earlier in this chapter. We will now look at a collaborative response to lower priority behaviours. These are behaviours that we may want to change but are not rated as areas to focus on at this time.

### Adjusting expectations

There are a range of school experiences that we recognise are hard for some children with PDA to tolerate. In these cases we need to think carefully about why and how often we are putting them in challenging situations. Once we have identified that a particular issue is not a high priority it would be wise to limit their exposure to known triggers. This doesn't mean that we are not working towards extending their tolerance in the future. It means that we are making balanced, collaborative decisions about matching their current tolerance and the coping skills they have with the demands of the situation or task.

For instance, a pupil may find eating in the dinner hall so fraught that they are unable to eat a reasonable lunch and are getting involved in conflict with other pupils that can carry on through the afternoon. Put in a priority rating chart it might look like Table 4.10.

Table 4.10 doesn't mean that we lose sight of reintegrating Lucas slowly and carefully at some point. It is a preventative strategy for now.

**Table 4.10 Priority rating chart example 3**

| How important is it that Lucas... | Priority level | Comments, rationale and plan |
|---|---|---|
| Eats lunch in the dining hall at the same time as the other children | Low | It is important that he manages to eat a reasonable amount of food since he doesn't cope well when he is hungry. He currently finds it overwhelming to be in the sensory and social environment of the dining hall. |
| | | Lucas's lunch to be provided in the library den just next to the dining room. He is to have access to school lunch menu but can supplement this with packed lunch items if there is not enough he will eat. He will be supported by either Miss Evans or Mr Swartz. |
| | | Over time and on more positive days he will be encouraged to keep the library door open, to chat about what can be seen happening in the dining hall and to return his tray to the dining hatch. |
| Completed in consultation with... | Date | Review of the above planned for... |

## Distraction

Distracting a child is a valid response to a lower priority behaviour. It might involve using a favourite activity, humour or a surprise. The intention is to alter the mood and guide the child back to a preferable way of behaving. The purpose is to avoid a flashpoint and to keep the child engaged with something positive. For example, a pupil who has difficulty with the transition home at the end of the school day may benefit from having the usual expectations lifted for a while. They may find it very hard to organise their bags and coat, tidy up the classroom and wait in a busy sensory and social environment. It may work better for them that just before the end of the day they are given an errand or a motivating activity. This could lead them to a quieter exit where their personal items are located and from where their carer can collect them smoothly.

### Planned ignoring

This means actively deciding not to react to certain behaviours even if the child knows they are provocative. It means that while upholding the agreed high priorities you ignore lower level disruption or irritants as part of your plan. For instance, during the time you are settling a child into a new classroom you may plan to ignore the less than polite way they ask for things. This is not what you expect of them long term and may not match what you expect of the other children, but for now it is something you will let go.

### Legitimising the behaviour

A child may repeatedly leave the classroom, maybe finding bogus or disruptive reasons to do so. You could try giving them a valid reason to do so. You could ask them to take a message to the school office before they feel the need to leave the class anyway. This gives them the exit they require, offers them a movement break to keep them regulated and legitimises a behaviour that is otherwise problematic.

### Choices and alternatives

Children with PDA respond well when they have a sense of control and influence. You may give children choices about details, for example, do you want to use the atlas or Google Earth? Or you can refer to personalised work, for example, do you want to do your project on Championship football teams or Minecraft®? The number of choices offered needs to match the child's ability, their understanding and tolerance. In addition, choices can work well if they are presented in an indirect visual way which provides more thinking time. Some school staff can feel frustrated about giving pupils more control than is typical in a classroom setting. It should be remembered, however, that it is the adult who remains in control of which and how many options the child has access to.

 ## Manage meltdowns

Children with PDA are vulnerable to overload. This might be in response to the demands of the social situation, their mood and their sensory sensitivities, all of which add to their high anxiety. Children with PDA who become overloaded are easily tipped beyond what they can tolerate, which can lead to meltdowns.

Meltdowns are significantly different to tantrums. Tantrums tend to be goal oriented. Tantrums happen in order for the child to get the thing they want which means they have a focus and a plan, require an audience. Tantrums are an angry or frustrated outburst with a purpose. Meltdowns are different to this.

Meltdowns are a response to being overwhelmed. Meltdowns can be explosive or be a shutdown. Meltdowns are not a deliberate action in order to make something happen or change. They are an emotional, anxiety-driven reaction to being overloaded. They are extremely distressing to the person experiencing them as well as to those witnessing and supporting them. Fear is the primary driver behind a meltdown, which explains how they are linked to the flight, fight or freeze responses. Meltdowns are sometimes likened to a panic attack.

During meltdowns children are likely to experience:

- raised anxiety

- physical symptoms of fear, for example, palpitations, sweating, nausea

- limited awareness of their surroundings

- lower ability to process information

- lower ability to communicate

- increased risk of harming themselves, others or equipment

- increased likelihood of getting into conflict

- lower ability to make choices or to reason.

Not all children will experience meltdowns in the same way, but some comments that young people have made about their meltdowns include:

'It's like I have a storm inside my tummy that gets bigger and faster and I can't think about anything else but getting away from it.'

'I feel sweaty and my heart is racing and I get a sort of prickly feeling in my head like there's too much stuff poking at my brain.'

'There's something pushing in on me. Squashing me and trapping me. I feel like I need to escape or I will explode. If I can't get away I start to implode.'

'I feel like I am sinking. I usually lie on the floor and I cry. I don't want to be left on my own because I'm scared. But I don't want anyone to talk to me or ask me to do anything. I want to be with someone who I like. Someone who will sit with me and squeeze my hand and arm when I put it out to them. When it's over I am really tired and thirsty.'

As discussed in Chapter 2, it is really important that we understand *why* a child is behaving in a certain way rather than just describing *what* they are doing. Sadly we will not be able to avoid all meltdowns for the children we are supporting. However, we can hope to minimise them, not only by gaining a better understanding of the individual child but also by raising our awareness of potential triggers for a particular pupil. We can work on developing ways of spotting the signs of increased agitation as they present in individual children. This is why it is so important that adults communicate with each other to share their knowledge of the child and where input from parents who have learned to 'read' their children is crucial.

Earlier in this chapter we highlight key factors in managing the safety of children and those around them when they are in explosive situations. Some children shut down or implode. These children present less of a safety risk to their immediate environment, however they are still experiencing a version of the same emotional overload. These children may need slightly different support but the root of their meltdown needs the same understanding and careful response. The anxiety and emotional distress in children who shutdown is equally significant.

One teacher commented on a teenage boy with PDA being taught in a specialist setting:

When Harry first joined the school one of our biggest challenges was his explosive behaviour. Over time we have built good relationships with him and in the main we manage his anxiety well. There are still times when things get difficult, though nowadays he tends to shutdown instead. This is easier to deal with from a safety point of view. But we do not overlook the fact that, for him, the same feelings of being overwhelmed are happening. We try to make sure that staff are aware of the signals he gives out. There seems to be a pattern of escalating signs. It starts with him going a bit quiet and his shoulders sort of sink. Next, he puts his hood up and sometimes closes his eyes. This is when we really need to reach him. If we haven't been able to he then rests his head on the table, he may push items off the table or slide under the table himself. It can take a long time, sometimes a couple of hours, to re-engage him if he reaches this point.

Harry himself commented:

Sometimes I explode and sometimes I implode. I used to explode more than I do now that I'm older. Inside, I still have a lot of the same feelings, it's just that they come out in a different way. When I explode it can be dangerous and it's exhausting. I feel panicky and I don't know what to do to make it better. When I shutdown it's safer and more boring but I still feel panicky and don't know what to do. With both types of meltdown when it's over it can be hard to remember what happened and why it happened.

Meltdowns can be upsetting and exhausting for everyone involved and time needs to be made to help all parties recover. The children may need physical and emotional recovery time. The adults may also benefit from some time away from the situation to regroup and later on to debrief and support each other.

Part of this recovery should include time to repair relationships with the child, which might have sustained damage during the meltdown. Positive relationships between these children and the adults who support them are so important that in most cases this repair should be the priority. The adults who are most effective at supporting pupils with PDA are those with strong positive relationships with them; who are there for them on their best days and their worst days; who are able to move on from difficult incidents without judgement. That does not mean that there are no consequences following an incident. It means that the consequences are characterised by understanding not by judgement. There may be natural consequences following an incident, such as not being able to use an iPad because it was damaged.

Sanctions do not tend to work well for children with PDA and are especially unhelpful as a response to a meltdown, which children on overload cannot help.

 ## Promote self-awareness, emotional wellbeing and personalising learning

Prioritising social and emotional wellbeing provides a key component of individualised support for pupils with PDA. Designing a personalised curriculum to meet the educational needs of pupils with PDA should include aspects not only of their academic learning but also of their broader social, independence and engagement skills. Indeed, these are such significant elements of a successful educational experience for children that we have dedicated chapters 6 and 7 to providing further detail of these core strategies of Collaborative Approaches to Learning.

 ## Adjust the use of rewards and sanctions

Many school settings have systems for praising and rewarding children. These are for very understandable and laudable reasons. However, praise does not always work in the way it was intended for pupils with PDA. Children with PDA can feel extremely uncomfortable when they are praised for doing well. There could be a number of reasons behind this. One young person said:

> I don't like it when Mr Abbot says I've done some good work. It makes me feel a mixture of shy, nervous and cross... I feel shy that everyone will look at me and expect me to do or say the right thing and I usually don't know what that is. I feel nervous because I don't want him to start expecting me to do work that good every day... and I feel cross because I had been enjoying that work and now he's spoiled it.

Many pupils with PDA respond better to an individualised form of praise. One teacher developed a coded signal of asking her pupil with PDA if she could borrow her pencil sharpener when she wanted to indicate that she was praising his work. Other pupils respond well to praise being given indirectly, such as commenting on a good piece of work a pupil has done to another child or teacher but in the hearing of the pupil with PDA. One teacher appealed to her pupil's sense of humour by putting fun Post-it® notes complimenting him in places only he would find.

Reward charts are intended to motivate pupils and celebrate their achievements. However, they can carry an implicit demand to do the thing the reward is aimed at before the child has even begun the session. For some children with PDA this represents a demand from the outset. In addition we have to think about how motivating the reward we are offering an individual is for them.

A child who was in a class where there was a reward system which displayed charts for each pupil on the classroom wall described the difficulties for him:

> I only like to be in the top 5 of the star charts. If I'm not near the top I get really upset about that and I can't stop thinking about it. I wish no one else could see my chart. That would be less stressful... Plus, I think it's very unfair that other children get stickers for doing things that I could easily do. I have to do really hard work to get my stickers... I don't want the prizes anyway.

It is obviously important if we use reward systems that they achieve what they are intended for. That is to encourage, motivate and celebrate. Rewards need to be tailored not only regarding the actual prizes on offer but also how the system is structured. A rewarding prize for a child with PDA may need to be different from what other pupils in class receive. Successful examples have included time to knit, vacuum, play cricket, cook, as well as to earn a tangible item such as a magazine, new wristbands or posters.

Many schools have identified activities that pupils enjoy which also regulate them. It is always good to know what these activities are and to include them in a child's school experience. However, it is not advisable to link these regulating activities to a reward system. Children should have frequent, easy access to activities that keep them calm and engaged. Otherwise the very day that a child needs regulating most is the day that they are least likely to earn the activity that helps them regulate.

Schools understandably also use sanctions as a means of managing pupil behaviour. They are also intended to act as a deterrent. Sanctions work for children who understand consequences and are able to keep their impulses in check. They work for children who want social approval and know how to go about achieving that. They work for children who seek to avoid feeling disappointed in themselves or embarrassed. They work for children who can predict outcomes in a range of situations.

If we remind ourselves of the key characteristics of PDA, we note that we are supporting pupils who have difficulty, amongst other things, with:

- understanding emotions

- understanding consequences

- controlling impulses

- repairing social relationships

- taking responsibility for their own actions

- connecting with a sense of pride or shame.

Children and young people with PDA don't always make the links between their own actions and the consequences that follow. Combined with the difficulties above this goes some way to explaining why sanctions tend not to be effective for pupils with PDA.

That doesn't mean that you are not able to teach these skills or that the children are unable to learn them. It does mean that we shouldn't make assumptions about their learning in this respect. It means that they may learn these skills later and that they will need specifically teaching.

You could try using strategies like drawing as part of a debrief with a child following a tricky situation. Flow charts or other diagrams can also be useful to demonstrate options or likely outcomes of certain choices, as in Figure 4.1.

Sometimes children with PDA can respond to the pressure of a threatened sanction by 'outmanoeuvering' the adult, in effect removing the impact of the sanction. For example:

Teacher: 'If you don't get changed out of your PE kit you won't be able to have time to go on the computer next lesson.'

Pupil: 'I don't care. I don't want to go on the computer now. The games you have at school are boring anyway.'

Interactions like this don't leave the teacher much room for negotiation about that particular matter. They can leave teachers feeling exposed in front of other pupils but they do show us something about the child as well. Questions to reflect upon include: To what degree do you feel the child is genuinely bored by what you are trying to present as a motivator? What is their understanding of the impact of this sort of negotiating? What is their understanding of the consequences, that is, are they really not going to mind missing computer time when the time comes?

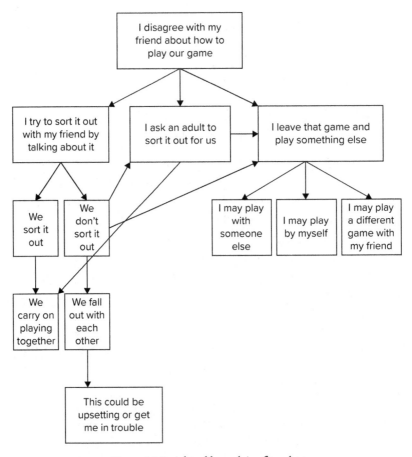

*Figure 4.1 Social problem-solving flow chart*

Some children will test whether you will actually see through what you threaten. Don't be surprised if this happens. Do be sure that this issue is sufficiently important. Remember that you will all be dealing with the consequences, not only the child. This is not to say that we should let absolutely anything go for the sake of short-term peace. It does mean we 'choose our battles' wisely. For example, getting into conflict about wearing full school uniform could have problematic results. If responses for an individual child could include physical damage, school refusal or non-attendance at an exam we have to consider our priorities.

You can use naturally occurring outcomes instead of sanctions. These can teach the principles of consequences without the element of threat. For example:

> 'I'm afraid we can't get the balls out at playtime today. Do you remember you threw the shed key in the pond yesterday? We have to wait until the caretaker comes to fit a new lock tomorrow.' (Note: this may be a point you want to make to the child even if you do actually have a spare key.)

Building on your understanding of the key strategies that are set out in this chapter the proforma in Table 4.11 provides a prompt for making adaptations to your everyday approach. (A downloadable version is available in the Appendix.)

It is not intended to be yet another piece of paperwork that should be completed on a day-to-day basis. It is intended as a check-in or reminder. When school staff are new to supporting a pupil with PDA it can be a tool that for a time they find helpful to keep to refer to and to use as a framework when discussing classroom practice.

**Table 4.11 Maximising participation prompt sheet**

| THIS IS THE TASK... |  |
| --- | --- |
| (this may be an everyday task, a piece of work, a new activity, etc.) |  |
| **How can I increase participation by considering...?** |  |
| What adaptations can I make to the environment? |  |
| What adaptations can I make to the group? The seating plan? |  |
| How would it be helpful for me to introduce the task? |  |
| Is this task an agreed priority? |  |
| What motivators would be helpful? |  |
| How should we deploy the staff available? |  |
| How can I adjust the expectations? (not only by reducing them) |  |
| What opportunities for choice can I offer? |  |
| What opportunities can I offer for building on the pupil's strengths or interests? |  |
| How will it be helpful to respond if the task goes well? |  |
| How will it be helpful to respond if the task does not go well? |  |

## Summary

The strategies in this chapter provide guidance on how to support pupils with PDA in everyday practice. They should be read in conjunction with the principles of Collaborative Approaches to Learning outlined in Chapter 3. They should also be seen in the context of the characteristics of the condition covered in Chapter 1. Doing so will ensure that as practitioners we don't only *use approaches that are effective* but that we *have an understanding of why they are effective.* This will mean we are better able to adapt them to other pupils we work with in the future. It will also make it easier for us to explain our rationale to other colleagues, which will promote collaboration and help us coach less experienced staff.

In describing the Collaborative Approaches to Learning approach, we are not suggesting that there is one set of strategies for all pupils with PDA and a separate set for all pupils with a more straightforward presentation of autism. We are suggesting that a particular emphasis is needed to support pupils with PDA. This different emphasis should be characterised by:

- carefully chosen priorities

- indirect approaches

- collaborative decision making

- making adjustments and accommodations

- providing additional processing time

- using flexible, creative and novel approaches

- managing confrontation, rewards and boundaries with care

- promoting emotional wellbeing

- personalising learning.

Chapters 6 and 7 build on the themes of personalising curriculum and promoting emotional wellbeing in more detail.

## Chapter 5

# GETTING STARTED

Although of course every child with PDA is very individual, this chapter outlines some common themes in effectively supporting these pupils, whether they are new to your class or whether it is time to review and reframe how you work with them. We will introduce some considerations and then go on to cover key points to build into settling a child with PDA into your setting.

## Key considerations

### Consider what's gone before for the family

If a child is starting new at your school, it is often the case that their family has already had a complicated and sometimes negative experience of previous education placements for their child. Maybe their child's needs have not been accommodated as they would have liked in the past, their child may have been through a breakdown in their school placement, and families may feel disappointed with the support they have had. Alternatively, maybe their child's needs have been met very well at a previous school and the family is nervous that a new placement/class/member of staff may not be able to do so as effectively. These scenarios understandably leave families feeling anxious, which is why making time to listen to them, to acknowledge their experiences and to build good relationships with school staff is crucial.

> He is about to start his third school in four years. We are hopeful this will be the right one for him and that he can at last enjoy going to school and start to make progress once more. I have to admit that I am also a bit worried for myself about finding the energy for going through the whole process of getting to know new staff and trusting them with my son all over again.

One parent described it:

> There are likely to be a number of other people who know the child coming to your classroom well. This includes their family, adults who have worked with them previously and other professionals who may have identified certain aspects of their profile. Even if a child's previous placement was not successful and you have no intention of repeating some of the strategies used there, finding out about them will give you a picture of the child's experience of that period of their life and will help you appreciate whether there are preconceptions they may be bringing to their new setting.

Reflecting on preparing to settle a pupil with PDA into her mainstream class a teacher said:

> I'm so glad that we made the time to get to know her family at the same time that we were getting to know her. During those first delicate weeks settling her into school after she had hardly been out of her bedroom for six months it proved invaluable to be able to pick up the phone regularly and discuss with her mum how we were going to manage everyday situations together that we were new to understanding.

### Consider what's gone before for the child

Children with PDA may have had a difficult time at school in the past. They might feel anxious about everyday classroom activities as well as even attending on a regular basis. They may have had specific experiences that have left them feeling resistant or overwhelmed about certain aspects of school. They may be nervous about relationships with school staff or with pupils. They may have particular sensitivities to many ordinary experiences that are part of going to school. The child might have had a period of time out of school altogether and become unfamiliar with the ordinary routines and everyday systems of school life. On the other hand they may also have learned that certain explosive behaviours can create dramatic or avoidant effects.

### Build rapport and alliance with the child's family

Collaboration is at the heart of meeting the needs of pupils with PDA, and building a positive relationship with the family underpins this way of working. Often before professionals meet a child they begin contact with the child's family, which represents an opportunity to learn about the history and character of the pupil you are trying to get to know. In the same way that we recognise a child's perspectives and experiences, it is also crucial to do the same with regard to the family. Each family has its own 'personality' and in order to work together positively professionals need to understand the character of the families they support. Moreover, it is not unusual for children with PDA to present very differently at home to how they are at school, so we need to build a holistic picture of each individual. School provides only a part of the child's day and it can often make a crucial difference if staff appreciate the issues associated with that child getting ready to come to school in the first place, alongside other factors which also affect many other pupils on the autism spectrum such as supply teachers, school trips, new uniform, homework and so on.

### Build rapport and alliance with the child

Following these early steps it is important to take time to build a positive relationship with the child: one in which they feel valued, listened to and accepted. It should not be assumed that this will match the typical teacher–pupil interaction common in most classrooms. The guiding principle here is about creating rapport and a sense of alliance between the pupil and the staff who support them. This positive relationship then becomes a tool in itself to promote engagement and co-operation, to reduce anxiety and to help children move on from difficult incidents.

Activities in the early stages are best based on building trust and respect. Tasks are most successful if they are centred on the pupil's interests. Raised anxiety is usually the biggest single obstacle these children face in relation to them being able to participate, co-operate and learn. For some this anxiety will affect them even being able to attend school in the first place, so every day that a pupil leaves school wanting to come back the following day is an excellent way to reinforce that school is a motivating and worthwhile place to be. To this end, using humour and fun activities, keeping the length and intensity of sessions within the child's comfort zone and giving them opportunities for regulating activities are all key factors in a successful start to a new school, staff team or class base.

### Observe and listen

This is one of the key principles of Collaborative Approaches to Learning, as explained in Chapter 3. It applies not only while you are getting started with a pupil but in an ongoing way. Observing and listening to the child, as well as to others who may have differing experiences of the same child, will provide helpful understanding of what makes sense *of* this child and of what makes sense *to* this child.

School environments are very busy places and school staff easily become swept up in 'doing'. The benefits of observing should not be underestimated. We can learn a lot from watching and listening to a child and we can also learn some useful skills from observing how others interact with them. We can take note of the impact of their environment and of the social and emotional context of the situation. We need not only to *identify* what we have seen but also to *interpret* what we have seen to try to understand *why* something has occurred. Our aim is to understand what is driving the child's thinking and behaviour.

In our observations, as well as looking at what the child is doing (or is avoiding doing), we can learn more about them by noticing what they could be doing but aren't. For example, the child who refuses to sit at the table with a TA to complete an activity, insisting that they are too busy sorting out their LEGO® pieces, but who is meanwhile answering questions correctly about the work task is actually participating to a degree. They *could* be sitting at a table completing the task independently, but then again they *could be* refusing altogether, they *could* have left the room and so on. Ideally we would like to continue working towards the child feeling more able to engage in a more direct way that is typical of classroom behaviour, but it gives us a positive starting point if we can recognise participation wherever it can be achieved.

## Settling a child in

Settling a child into a new setting will require staff and families to think carefully about some of the following:

- **Time of day**. When you are settling a child into a new placement think about whether they are ready for a full day or a phased start. If they are having a phased start, which part of the school day is most likely to carry the best chances of engagement and how long should a session be? If they are attending for part of a day, how will you support them when it's time to leave? What can you do to help them feel as emotionally regulated as possible just after they arrive and just before they have to transition to home? How will you balance giving them social as well as other learning opportunities without overloading them? Is it best to include a lunch break or to avoid the dining room experience in the very early stages?

- **Choosing staff**. Consider a suitable and positive personality match. Which member of staff is most likely to work effectively and build rapport with this particular child? Will this member of staff be the lead in liaising with the family? Who will be the nominated co-ordinator to work together with family and other professionals involved? Are there any other professionals who need to be included in the pupil's placement and target setting? How and when can you extend the initially small team who work closely with the pupil? When this happens how do you support, guide and liaise with these members of staff?

- **Environment.** Children and young people with PDA may be sensitive to certain sensory environments, may have personal preferences and may be distracted in various circumstances. Given that we are aiming at maximum learning and engagement alongside minimal anxiety it is worth giving consideration to the broader environment and the demands implicit within it. Particularly think about these issues for children who may have been out of school for some time, so have become unaccustomed to school routines such as lining up, sitting on the carpet in class, assembly, using school toilets, dining rooms, PE halls and so on.

- **Content of tasks and activities.** All pupils learn best when they are engaged with the work tasks but for children with PDA this engagement is particularly vital. Factors such as helping them achieve a state of manageable anxiety and arousal levels, supporting them with positive relationships and creating a suitable environment provide the basics. Then we have to think about the style and content of the activities we present. Work will need to appeal to pupils with PDA not only because the content captures their interest but also because you have presented it in an indirect, flexible way with opportunities for making choices, for humour, to put work on pause and to creatively amend it.

- **Managing boundaries.** Choosing priorities is a core factor in managing children with PDA. This issue was explored in more detail in Chapter 4. One of the important questions for staff to ask themselves is, 'What are the absolute non-negotiables and what are the preferable but flexible expectations?' Equally, which are the issues that at these early stages are simply not priorities (this doesn't mean they will never be, but that a conscious decision not to focus on them for now has been made). Making these decisions is certainly best done collaboratively.

- **Reducing stress and feeling at ease.** All children do best if they feel that they are understood and accepted for who they are. Children with PDA have particularly fragile emotional wellbeing and self-esteem. Sensitivity and mood in children with PDA can be extremely variable from day to day, from session to session and from setting to setting. Reducing anxiety will play a huge role in helping to keep these children regulated and engaged. It will also create opportunities to learn. Within the context of trusted relationships children with PDA can be encouraged to explore personalised themes about self-awareness and emotional problem-solving. Simple considerations for staff include, for example: Can this child bring a favoured toy from home? Can they have time and space in a preferred area with a special interest to keep them regulated? Should we use additional stress-relieving activities which appeal to them? If so when, where and with whom do these fit into their time at school? Are there sensory input activities which will support their optimum arousal levels? How do we communicate with other staff about how best to promote their emotional wellbeing? How do we determine priorities to develop in their learning in this respect?

- **Gauging the child's understanding.** It is going to be important to try as early as possible to get a gauge of the child's genuine understanding. Often children with PDA show a surface sociability that misleads those around them regarding their genuine level of understanding. It is important not to make assumptions about this. This means that we need to determine a realistic level of understanding in the child so that we can adapt the style and pace of our communication appropriately. It can be helpful to provide children with PDA visual supports in as much as they provide clear and concrete communication. However, children with PDA will need a different emphasis and approach to using visual strategies which incorporates elements of choice. This is in order to avoid presenting them with an overly direct list of perceived demands.

- **Preparation.** Children with PDA who are anxious and avoidant are likely to respond well when they are aware of what is happening around them and comfortable with what is being asked of them. They may benefit from a degree of preparation in advance for preparing them for a new experience of school such as the people they may meet, the buildings, the travel and toilet arrangements and so on. However, too much preparation can backfire with some children and young people with PDA because it can be perceived as pressure or demands or because it gives sufficient information that can then be used strategically to avoid the expectation. It is a delicate and very personalised balance to achieve and professionals do well to take advice from families about how much advance preparation is helpful and how much the 'surprise factor' can be effective too.

- **Incorporate time for liaison and development.** A perennial challenge for any educational setting is creating and protecting discussion and liaison time. There are no easy answers for this dilemma, however difficulties can soon dominate if this time is not allocated. It is important to capture all the relevant perspectives in these regular discussions. This should include parental input and that of classroom staff as well as support from senior leaders or other professionals who understand why their staff will need to make the adaptations necessary to meet the needs of pupils with PDA. Staff will benefit from access to reputable training, from guidance or coaching and from recovery and debriefing time following more trying days or specific incidents.

- **Pace everyone's energy and stamina.** Limitless amounts of energy are not available to the child or any of the adults who are supporting them both in and outside school. Devise an integrated plan that is aspirational yet achievable but one that is also sustainable.

When asked what made a difference when they were settling a child into their specialist secondary school a TA said:

> Having tried to get her to attend school on a regular basis for nearly half a term, it was surprising how big a difference it made when we decided to 'let go' of lots of everyday expectations about the school day. Being able to adapt things like wearing correct uniform, lining up in the playground, basing her work on topics and games that matched her interests and being low key about homework were really important. These things made all the difference to school being a positive experience not only for her but also for the adults who were working with her.

Supporting a child with PDA to settle in your setting or school is not a straightforward task. It will require staff to work well with families, to have sufficient flexibility to amend timetables and usual school routines, to collaborate with everyone involved and to protect the emotional wellbeing of the child as well as the adults living and working with them. This is long-term work. On the other hand, sometimes it may initially seem that it has all gone surprisingly well until the 'honeymoon' period is over. That is why it is so important to have put the time and skill up front to build good relationships and experiences since you may need to rely on this positive history when difficulties arise. It is not unusual for pupils with PDA to have commented that their preferred members of staff are the ones who are there for them on their best days and their worst days...and as with any relationship this one will require reflection, maintenance and from time to time, repair. There is more detail about ways to support the adults who support the children with PDA in Chapter 9.

# Chapter 6

# PERSONALISING THE CURRICULUM

Chapter 4 on key strategies has outlined some of the ways in which activities might be presented to a child with PDA in an indirect, flexible and creative way so that this reduces their anxiety and increases their tolerance and engagement. Clearly, all pupils learn best when they are fully engaged, not only with the adults who are supporting them but also with the content of the activity that is presented. It is undoubtedly the case that with more complex and, at times, reluctant learners it is crucial to build on their strengths and interests and to involve them in decisions about their learning.

This rationale fits very well with the increasing emphasis given to person-centred planning in the Special Educational Needs and Disability Code of Practice (Department for Education/Department of Health (DfE/DoH) 2015). An important distinction needs to be drawn when thinking about outcomes and we need to consider what is *important to* the child or young person (what they themselves want to achieve) and what is *important for* them (as judged by others with their best interests at heart).

When thinking about what is important for pupils with PDA most teachers and parents, while valuing academic attainment, would see areas such as independence and social and emotional understanding as priorities. This would also be reflected in the views of most children and young people themselves. Indeed, the Preparing for Adulthood programme, funded by the Department for Education (2018), identifies four main outcomes based on what young people with disabilities say are important to them in order to lead full lives with choices about their future and control of their support. These are employment, independent living, community participation and health and are reiterated in the Code of Practice (DfE/DoH 2015). Research suggests, however, that adults with autism are far less likely to achieve these outcomes, and life chances can be severely limited in comparison with others (Pellicano 2014).

The Autism Education Trust (AET) was founded in 2007 and is partly funded by the DfE. Its purpose is to improve education support for all children and young people on the autism spectrum. To this end the AET has commissioned a number of research projects and has also developed training materials for educational practitioners, a set of national standards for settings to use, a competency framework for people working with school age pupils with autism and a progression framework to demonstrate progress in learners with autism. Throughout all of this material the themes of personalisation, pupil participation and building on strengths are emphasised.

One report, *Educational Provision and Outcomes for People on the Autism Spectrum* (Wittemeyer *et al.* 2011), described similar findings to the Preparing for Adulthood programme and one of their key recommendations was that guidance from the DfE should be provided to teachers especially those in mainstream settings, to support achieving a balance between teaching key academic skills with other skills which promote social and emotional skills as well as independence (Wittemeyer *et al.* 2011).

This chapter will look at some of the ways that might be helpful in planning the curriculum to make it meaningful and relevant for a child with PDA, plus how learning objectives can be chosen and balanced to meet individual needs.

## Designing a personalised curriculum

For a child with PDA a distinction may need to be made between differentiation and personalisation of the curriculum. Put simply, a *differentiated curriculum* takes a body of knowledge as its starting point which needs to be imparted to the learner, and it is the practitioner's task to find ways of making this accessible. On the other hand, a *personalised curriculum* takes the learner as its starting point and builds a curriculum around their individual needs and preferences, using this to maximise potential for engagement. The learner is involved in decisions about content, context and delivery of the curriculum which take into account their interests and learning style. The role of the adult is to guide the learner sensitively towards successful learning. David Hartley of Birmingham University writes:

> Personalisation differs from differentiation in that it affords the learner a degree of choice about what is learned, when it is learned and how it is learned. This may not indicate unlimited choice since learners will still have targets to be met and informed adults will wish to play a part in guiding the learner to make responsible choices. However, personalisation may also provide learners the opportunity to learn in ways that suit their individual learning styles and multiple intelligences. (2009, pp.2–3)

Involving the young person in the process of planning their curriculum can in itself reduce anxiety about loss of control and avoids them seeing the curriculum as something which is being 'imposed' on them. As well as being motivating and leading to increased engagement, involvement in this process can lead to improved confidence and self-esteem. This type of involvement in decision making has been highlighted by Public Health England as being beneficial to mental health.

> Involving students in decisions that impact on them can benefit their emotional health and wellbeing by helping them to feel part of the school and wider community and to have some control over their lives. (Public Health England 2015, p.14)

Promoting emotional wellbeing in children with PDA is discussed further in the next chapter.

Within the principles of person-centred planning advocated in the Code of Practice (DfE/DoH 2015) there is a delicate balance to aim at for those who 'guide' the learner in deciding what is *important to* and *important for* the child or young person. The implications of this mean we need to think carefully about:

- If 'important to' outweighs 'important for', the child has all choice but no responsibility which can be risky/unhealthy.

- If 'important for' outweighs 'important to' the child is safe and healthy at the expense of what they might want, choose or prefer.

- Getting the balance between 'important to' and 'important for' will mean that the child is happy, healthy, safe, engaged.

## Identifying priorities for learning

Taking into account what might be 'important *to*' and 'important *for*' a child or young person with PDA can provide a useful starting point for planning a personalised curriculum. Planning in this way involves identifying individual priorities and ways in which these needs might be met within the educational setting, that is, the types of experiences and activities to be provided.

Figure 6.1 provides an example of this type of planning for Grace, a 14-year-old with PDA. Grace is academically able in many aspects of her learning but has difficulty in accessing some of her lessons due to high anxiety and demand avoidance. She has a variety of sensory sensitivities which impact on her joining groups and attending sessions at a local college where she wants to study some of her GCSE subjects.

The individual priorities identified combine those of what is important *to* Grace (e.g. independence, choice, interests, relationships, qualifications) with those that are important *for* her as identified by those who know her well (e.g. reduced anxiety, increased confidence, co-operation, engagement). Once priorities have been agreed, activities and contexts that support learning in these areas can be identified. In Figure 6.1 these have been grouped under five broad headings which encompass needs arising from Grace's form of autism as well as her academic pathway. This information is then used to draw up a personalised timetable.

**Example for Grace**

**Social communication and interaction**

- Personal Tutorials
- Language and interaction groups
- Clubs and interest groups
- Breaks and lunchtimes
- Flexible grouping

**Emotional wellbeing and keeping healthy and safe**

- Personal hygiene/care
- Personal, social, health and economic education (PSHE)/Sex education
- Personal Tutorials
- Physical activity/PE
- Routines and mealtimes
- E-safety
- Community visits
- Motivators and special interests

**Independence and community participation**

- College
- Work experience
- Clubs
- Independent study
- Use of leisure time
- Community visits/Shopping
- Person-centred planning

**National Curriculum and accreditation**

- KS4 curriculum including qualifications (GCSEs)
- Interests and strengths
- Choices

**Learning skills**

- Motivation and engagement
- Independent learning
- Organisation and planning
- Developing skills and strengths
- Evaluating own learning

**Sensory and physical needs**

- Awareness and management of own sensory needs

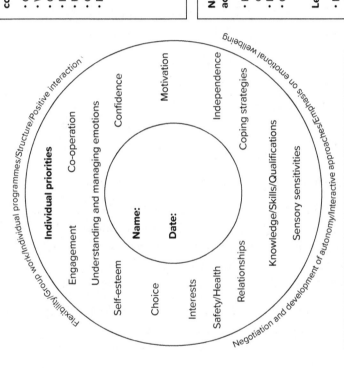

Flexibility/Group work/Individual programmes/Structure/Positive interaction

**Individual priorities**

Engagement   Co-operation

Understanding and managing emotions

Confidence

Motivation

Self-esteem

Choice

Interests

Safety/Health   Relationships

Knowledge/Skills/Qualifications

Sensory sensitivities

Coping strategies

Independence

**Name:**

**Date:**

Negotiation and development of autonomy/Interactive approaches/Emphasis on emotional wellbeing

*Figure 6.1 Planning a personalised curriculum*

These elements of her curriculum were then incorporated into her school timetable.

The first timetable, Table 6.1, shows the scheduled lessons which make up the basis of Grace's week. What is important to note is that behind this seemingly simple schedule lies a great deal of planning, flexibility and adaptation on the part of staff in order to support Grace's engagement and attendance.

Table 6.1 Grace's organisational timetable (1)

| Day | | Session 1 | | Session 2 | | Session 3 | Session 4 |
|---|---|---|---|---|---|---|---|
| Monday | T | Personal Tutorial | B | ICT | L | Work-related learning | |
| Tuesday | U | Maths | R | English | U | PE (off site) | |
| Wednesday | T | Science | E | Science | N | PSHE | Art |
| Thursday | O | Girls Group | A | English | C | History | DT |
| Friday | R | English | K | Maths | H | Yoga | Independent study |

Factors taken into account when drawing up Grace's timetable include:

- ensuring a balance of academic 'syllabus-led' activities with those that allow Grace more choice or control of what she is learning and where expectations can be lowered, for example, qualifications-led work (maths, English, science) balanced by non-accredited options based on Grace's interests (history, art)

- opportunities for social and emotional development supported by skilled staff with whom she has a longstanding relationship (e.g. a mentoring session, Personal Tutorial or Girls Group)

- working in partnership with Grace around contexts for learning; for example, work-related learning and PE sessions were negotiated with Grace and took account of her interests, preferences and sensory processing issues.

The second timetable, Table 6.2, provides a more detailed account of some of the adaptations made.

**Table 6.2 Grace's adapted timetable (2)**

| Day | | Session 1 | | Session 2 | | Session 3 | Session 4 |
|---|---|---|---|---|---|---|---|
| **Monday** <br> *Flexible arrival time 9–9:30 and regulating activities on arrival* | T | **Personal Tutorial** <br> *With designated senior member of staff with longstanding relationship. Flexible context, e.g. cafe, charity shop, Games Workshop®* | B | **ICT** <br> *Taught in a small group but centred around personal interests. Flexible context, E-safety a priority via non-directive approaches* | L | **Work-related learning** | *Venue changed in response to sensory overload at first choice (i.e. G expressed preference for library over charity book shop)* |
| **Tuesday** <br> *Flexible arrival time and regulating activities* | U | **Maths** <br> *Following GSCE curriculum using adapted materials and supported by familiar, skilled staff. Learning breaks/self-regulation opportunities available as needed* | R | **English** <br> *Following GCSE curriculum. Choices given where possible, e.g. set texts. Flexible context for learning, i.e. with group or individual study (supported by TA) depending on levels of anxiety* | U | **PE** <br> *Taught off site at teenage gym facility with three peers. Sessions at school had not been successful* | **Art** <br> *Individualised projects focused on therapeutic benefit* |
| **Wednesday** <br> *Flexible arrival time and regulating activities* | T | **Science** <br> *Following BTEC curriculum at local college with her classmates. G travelled separately in staff car not in minibus so as to allow calmer journey and more flexible departure time* | E | **Science** <br> *During science session G supported by her personal tutor and senior member of staff due to positive relationship and to support risk assessment* | N | **PSHE** <br> *Prioritising areas such as personal safety and relationships and sex education* | |
| **Thursday** <br> *Flexible arrival time and regulating activities* | O | **Girls Group** <br> *Allowing G to form relationships with girls from other classes within a structured situation. G involved in choosing discussion topics* | A | **English** <br> *As above* | C | **History** <br> *A non-GCSE session allowing G to be involved in choosing content in a subject which she enjoys* | **D/T** <br> *Individualised projects based on interests facilitating business enterprise goods to sell* |
| **Friday** <br> *Flexible arrival time and regulating activities* | R | **English** <br> *A more flexible session which allows G to be involved in choosing content or to do 'homework' for GCSE sessions* | K | **Maths** <br> *As above* | H | **Yoga** <br> *Working with G to develop her own individualised yoga routine* | **Independent study** <br> *Opportunities to catch up with unfinished course work, and additional informal Personal Tutorial* |

## Project-based curriculum

Another example of personalised curriculum planning is to use a project-based or topic approach focused around personal interests to engage a child in learning in a motivating and meaningful way. An account of using this type of approach is described in Christie *et al.* (2012), where the topic of 'The Romans' is used as the starting point for planning a range of activities for an 11-year-old pupil named Duncan who had recently moved to a specialist school after the breakdown of his mainstream placement.

In order to engage Duncan, staff planned a series of cross-curricular learning tasks based on Duncan's own suggestions of aspects of the topic that interested him. Their role was to facilitate his research and recording within tasks which included activities such as telling the time using a sundial, researching and cooking Roman recipes, investigating Roman life and class structure, experiments based around the theme of volcanoes and art work using mosaic designs.

Throughout these activities staff adopted a low-key attitude and an emphasis on having fun. Duncan felt that he was able to guide the line of research and any ensuing projects. The role of staff was to sensitively ease his path through investigations, taking care to keep the balance between encouraging him to stay motivated and on task on the one hand (often by doing his least favoured part of the work such as writing), while trying to stretch his co-operation and knowledge on the other.

The personalised curriculum plan for Duncan below shows how this project takes into account his preferences and potential for engagement in relation to content, delivery and learning context. In addition, although the topic chosen is not 'labelled' as relating to specific subject work, it is clear that many opportunities for learning across a range of curriculum areas are present. In order to provide evidence of subject learning, outcomes should be identified by staff and individual progress recorded.

The learner is offered:

• Choice (what, when, how, where)
• Personal interests
• Support from trusted adult(s)
• Individual learning style

**What?**

• Roman diet/manners
• Pompeii
• Volcanoes
• Sundials
• Homes

**Curriculum areas covered**

• History
• Maths
• Literacy
• ICT
• Food tech
• Science
• Geography
• Art
• PSHE

Staff provide:

• Facilitated learning
• Various recording methods
• Guided support towards success
• Background work to support the timetable and curriculum

**How?**

• Missions and challenges
• Experiments
• Research/Enquiry
• Interviews
• Discussion
• Surveys
• Art and craft

**When/Where?**

• In and out of classroom
• Flexible timetabling
• Choice of activity

*Figure 6.2 Example of personalising the curriculum using
Duncan's chosen topic of 'The Romans'*

A downloadable blank version of this chart is available in the Appendix.

Although Figure 6.2 uses as its starting point a known interest of the child, young people with PDA are often curious and enquiring and may equally be engaged by a subject that is new to them. In addition, young people may 'move on' from previous special interests so it is important to ensure that staff knowledge of the child's preferences is up to date. As with the above, ensuring a degree of choice (either between or within topics) and using Collaborative Approaches to Learning can lead to engagement with a range of subject areas.

This can be seen in the following example, where a pupil, Arron, became very engaged with a unit of work planned around the popular children's book *Billionaire Boy* by David Walliams (Walliams 2011).

Arron initially 'opted out' of the session which he perceived as 'literacy work' and some alternative activities were made available to him at his individual table. He was, however, within sight and earshot of the lesson which included following the text of the book through an iPad attached to an interactive whiteboard. Arron soon began to show interest by making comments about the text and independently moved his chair so that he could be part of the group. He also volunteered his IT skills when the teacher was struggling to maintain the connection between the iPad and the board, allowing him a 'way in' to the session that was clearly valued and enhanced his status and self-esteem within the group. In addition to reading the book, pupils were offered a variety of activities linked to its content with which Arron became engaged. These included:

- quizzes on 'the story so far'
- making up an 'ideal timetable'
- 'What would you do with a billion pounds?' discussion activity
- designing and making an advert for a new chocolate bar
- making up a 'revolting school dinner' menu
- making posters about bullying
- memory games.

Throughout the activities Arron was supported by a familiar member of staff who provided non-directive prompts and scribed his ideas such as those for his 'Revolting Menu' below. Although reluctant to write himself, Arron contributed his ideas and was able to achieve a number of objectives related to the reading, comprehension and speaking and listening aspects of the unit of work.

## Arron's Revolting Menu

### Starters

Snail Soup

Hair Dumplings with Dandruff

### Main Courses

Fried Snake Steak

Dead Person Stew and Human Brain Dumplings

Perfectly Fried Panda

### Desserts

Sugared Human Hand with Gore of Honey Stuffing

Mouldy Ice Cream with Mouldy Chocolate Sauce

### Still Drinks

Cats' Mushed Guts

Blended Human Liver

### Fizzy Drinks

Rabbit Poo Coke

Gone-Off Fanta

### Hot Drinks

Blended Homer Simpson Drink

Blended Dog and Cat Coffee

Below is the teacher's summary of Arron's achievement at the end of the unit, showing how Arron has both engaged with the sessions and achieved a number of objectives specific to the literacy unit being taught:

Arron has had an excellent term in Literacy. He was very engaged with the text which he loved, really 'getting' the humour in it, and participated fully in sessions. Arron was able to recall in detail events in previous chapters and used this information to try and predict what might happen next. He was able to comment on characters and identify how different situations might make them feel. Arron enjoyed creative activities such as making up his own 'disgusting dinners' menu or designing a new chocolate bar. Although unwilling to write himself he dictated his ideas and contributed to illustrations.

This type of assessment is usually referred to as summative and is described in more detail in Chapter 8. Arron's achievements were recorded in Table 6.3.

Table 6.3 Literacy achievement record

|  | Achieved | Comment |
|---|---|---|
| **Speaking and listening** | | |
| Names and gives one attribute of a character | ✓ | Understood different attributes of key characters. |
| Recalls details from a story and communicates to others | ✓ | Excellent summary of previous events. |
| **Reading** | | |
| Uses context to help to decode text | ✓ | Evidence of this noted when reading from the whiteboard which reduced the direct demand for him. |
| Gives a simple description of a character from what has read | ✓ | Included good use of adjectives. |
| Describes an event from a story that has been read | ✓ | Used a range of low-demand activities to demonstrate, e.g. dictating, recording speech, drew cartoon strip. |
| Expresses an opinion of a character or a story line | ✓ | Formed his own ideas though didn't always pick up on 'hints' in text and needed additional prompts. Had clear views on credibility of storylines. |
| Makes a relevant comment about a feature of a story | ✓ | Showed that he could predict outcomes of a situation |
| Discusses how a character might act | ✓ | Described likely emotions of characters and had views about how they should/shouldn't react. |
| Discusses an incident in the text and comments on its effect on the story | ✓ | Demonstrated awareness of impact of events on the story and suggested alternative outcomes for different scenarios. |

| Writing | | |
|---|---|---|
| Talks to an adult about what they would like to write | ✓ | Able to express clear and well-formed ideas about what to write. |
| Able to put their ideas into writing using basic punctuation | ✓ | Dictated what he wanted to write to an adult and was able to correct adult's deliberate punctuation errors correctly. |

## Reflecting on using a personalised curriculum

To conclude this chapter, it is our experience that developing personalised curriculum plans for individual pupils can be a very effective way to meet the educational needs of pupils with PDA. However, doing so does require something of a shift in thinking for some classroom practitioners as well as for school leaders. This is not always straightforward and it is understandable that school staff and parents need time and careful thought to navigate this process successfully. It should become smoother with practice. As our schools continue to receive increasing numbers of complex pupils it is an approach that can be adapted to meet the needs of a wide range of young people.

Finally, it may be useful to reflect on a number of questions linked to personalising the curriculum as a means of evaluating practice in this area. These are included in a checklist (Table 6.4). A downloadable version is available in the Appendix.

- **Have we identified learning priorities?** How have we done this? Who has contributed to the discussion? (e.g. young person, parents)

- **Do the activities within the young person's timetable provide opportunities to address these learning priorities?**

- **Does the timetable take into account barriers to learning for this pupil?** Have we made sufficient adaptations to expectations? Environment? School rules/systems? Who is co-ordinating the timetable? Have decisions about adaptations been approved by those co-ordinating/overseeing the curriculum?

- **How are opportunities for engagement maximised?** Are we using opportunities for personal interest? Are teaching methods engaging? Are we offering opportunities for extending or offering new interests?

- **Who is involved in supporting the child?** Who is their trusted adult? Which peers do they identify as their friends?

- **Do we have sufficient resources to make a personalised curriculum work?** Space? Staffing? Materials? Subject knowledge?

- **Have we set learning outcomes that we can measure?** (i.e. academic and non-academic areas) How will we demonstrate progress? What kind of evidence will support our judgements? How will we use this information to inform our planning?

**Table 6.4 Personalised curriculum checklist**

| | |
|---|---|
| Have we identified learning priorities? How have we done this? Who has contributed to the discussion? (e.g. young person, parents) | |
| Do the activities within the young person's timetable provide opportunities to address these learning priorities? | |
| Does the timetable take into account barriers to learning for this pupil? Have we made sufficient adaptations to expectations? Environment? School rules/systems? Who is co-ordinating the timetable? Have decisions about adaptations been approved by those co-ordinating/overseeing the curriculum? | |
| How are opportunities for engagement maximised? Are we using opportunities for personal interests? Are teaching methods engaging? Are we offering opportunities for extending or offering new interests? | |

| | |
|---|---|
| Who is involved in supporting the child?<br><br>Who is their trusted adult?<br><br>Which peers do they identify as their friends? | |
| Do we have sufficient resources to make a personalised curriculum work?<br><br>Space?<br><br>Staffing?<br><br>Materials?<br><br>Subject knowledge? | |
| Have we set learning outcomes that we can measure? (i.e. academic and non-academic areas)<br><br>How will we demonstrate progress?<br><br>What kind of evidence will support our judgements?<br><br>How will we use this information to inform our planning? | |

Chapter 7

# ENCOURAGING SOCIAL UNDERSTANDING AND PROMOTING EMOTIONAL WELLBEING

There are a number of recurring themes throughout this book and one of the most notable is that of the need to promote social and emotional wellbeing for children and young people with PDA. There are likely to be some issues in these areas which will affect individuals differently. Different children will have their own sensitivities and may in addition be affected by other factors such as changes in family circumstances, puberty, moving schools and so on. We also need to take into account the impact that either well-managed or poorly regulated anxiety has on a child's mood, behaviour and ultimately on their learning.

## Encouraging social understanding

Children with PDA can come across as sociable yet they often experience underlying difficulties in developing and maintaining social relationships. It is important to keep in mind our understanding of the characteristics of PDA, as detailed back in Chapter 1, which will help us unpick the underlying source of these difficulties. Also, in Chapter 2 we outlined some of the implications for teaching and learning for pupils with PDA in respect of their social interactions. Building on our appreciation of this, we will now consider how we can facilitate more fully developed social understanding. This is not only a priority for the wellbeing of pupils with PDA but is a key aspect of their personalised curriculum.

Children with PDA are often very socially motivated and may seem to have an awareness of how others appear to feel. However, they may also have considerable difficulty with really understanding other people and relating to how they feel (in terms of empathy). They may also find it hard to use that understanding to maintain relationships (such as to realise when a relationship may benefit from some repair or a response may need an explanation).

They often express wanting to be at least as good as others, if not better, at a given activity. This has implications for their self-esteem. If they have a perfectionist nature with unrealistically high expectations of themselves, they may feel disappointed and may be put off trying something new. It can also have a negative impact on their social relationships in terms of how they accommodate, recognise and celebrate achievements in their peers, siblings or friends. They will need sensitively coaching through these issues.

It can be much harder to maintain a friendship than to start one. Conversation structures can be learned and shared interests can form the scaffold of many relationships. However, adjusting our responses in accordance with the moods, context and priorities of other people we spend time with is much more complicated. These are aspects of social relationships that are likely to present a challenge to many people with autism. They present a particular challenge to those with PDA because these are individuals who may be very sociable and able to recognise the feelings of other people on the one hand, yet on the other hand find social relationships confusing and exhausting, and when anxious are led to interact in a controlling manner which may inadvertently damage their relationships.

Children with PDA can, as mentioned earlier, develop strong opinions about other people. These may be strongly positive or negative. Different challenges can develop from both of these reactions which vary depending on whether they are directed towards another child or an adult.

## Positive 'social fixations'

Some children with PDA develop strong preferences for other people. If this is directed towards another child they can become rather controlling towards that other child and may try to limit the choices they make or the other children they can play with. In addition, some children with PDA, particularly girls, work so hard to emulate another person they have a positive fixation with that they can lose sight of their own authentic self in the process. They may be fixated with someone they know in real life, a fictional character or maybe a celebrity. When this occurs with another child it can have an aggravating impact on the child who is being so closely copied. It can also have a potentially negative impact on the child with PDA themselves because it may damage the very relationship they are working towards fostering.

Many children develop preferences for certain adults over others. It is not unusual to hear children with PDA described by school staff and parents as viewing the people who support them as either 'good or bad cop'. Some of the issues regarding being on the receiving end of a dislike are discussed in the next section. There are some obvious advantages if you have the 'good cop' role. You will be better able to connect with the pupil, to calm them, to talk about more difficult topics such as emotions, to achieve co-operation in teaching or advising them and to be able to uphold expectations of them which they are able to tolerate on the basis of the relationship. These positive relationships do not usually occur at random. They are born out of much time invested in building rapport and trust, however they are not immune to damage and will need to be repaired as necessary after difficult incidents.

In an annual review report a teacher reflected on some of the qualities noted in staff who worked well with 12-year-old Donny:

Donny shows clear preferences for certain staff members and responds well to these people. It has been crucial to build on these positive relationships as they are fundamental to helping him co-operate, negotiate, stay calm and learn. It has been important to try to widen the number of adults he is comfortable with so that the team supporting him can achieve a balance of making him feel secure whilst sharing the load of working so intensely with him. It is worth noting that common features these members of staff share are a creative, imaginative way of presenting tasks, a non-directive approach and an ability to move on from any difficult incidents without judgement.

As alluded to in this teacher's comments, in some cases these positive relationships can represent pressure for members of staff whose presence starts to be relied upon not only by the pupil but also by other staff. If this is not carefully managed it can mean that it is very hard for that adult to have enough time to attend meetings or training, or for them to have opportunities to work with other children. As outlined in Chapter 5, although when you are settling a child with PDA into your setting it can be wise to have one or two key adults with whom they can build rapport, it is equally unwise not to extend the team when possible so as to spread the load of expertise and energy.

### Negative 'social fixations'

Generally, it would be hoped that adults have 'broader shoulders' to accommodate the occasional ill-timed insult or put-down. Nonetheless we are all human and some of us might find this more challenging than others for a variety of reasons. There may be some occasions when a child with PDA takes a dislike to a member of staff following a previous conflict they had, or an incident when they felt misunderstood or misinterpreted. There may be others when the dislike is fuelled by something less rational such as what car they drive or whether they like a certain genre of music and so on. Although we should not be entirely surprised if a child with PDA takes a dislike to an adult who supports them, that doesn't mean that we have to accept any behaviour, such as insults or derogatory comments, without question. There is always scope for using these situations as teaching points. Adults who do and who don't have positive relationships with pupils with PDA play a significant role in modelling social accommodations and repair. For instance, you could find opportunities to demonstrate alternatives, or problem-solve by thinking out loud so that the child recognises the implications of their actions. This teaching can be covered both in real-time responses to incidents as well as in designated Personal Tutorials.

If the dislike is aimed at a particular pupil you will need to decide how to manage the situation in the best interests of all concerned. For example, where the other child's experience feels to them as though they are being negatively targeted, they may need to be taught some assertiveness and coping strategies which can be reinforced by staff. These strategies could include coaching the other pupils regarding recognising when they are being taken advantage of, learning a range of responses which can deflect put-downs, developing a bank of familiar adults who can support them, and asserting themselves positively rather than through their own behaviour. The child with PDA will need to develop an understanding of social and emotional consequences, to recognise the importance of making accommodations and managing impulsive behaviour, as well as about how having a negative impact on others can also bring negative outcomes for themselves.

Using emotional barometers, flow charts and spider diagrams can be helpful ways of representing this learning visually. Children with PDA may also respond well to acting out different scripts with puppets to explore themes of social consequences.

The drawing in Figure 7.1 provided a useful visual way to map the various factors that could be contributing to the sort of PE lesson Daniel had. Of course, this is not an exhaustive list and it needed adapting over time but it presented a concrete way to show that aspects of his friendships, his bodily feelings, his mood and what happens at home can all affect how he feels in school. Putting this on paper helped Daniel to understand some of the contributory factors of a wider context than simply what occurred in the lesson itself. It also supported him to start to make connections between different experiences. He added a further drawing using the metaphor of a podium to illustrate how he sometimes shifted from a good lesson to a bad one (Figure 7.2).

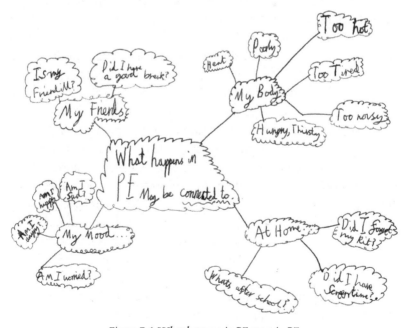

*Figure 7.1 What happens in PE stays in PE*

*Figure 7.2 Feel Good Inc.*

In terms of dealing with the everyday classroom situations where a child with PDA has developed a negative fixation with another pupil, it may be necessary to consider how often, for how long at a time and for which activities these children are together. We are not suggesting that these situations should be managed by simply avoiding putting children with PDA in contact with others they find hard to spend time with. We are suggesting that the risk of damage to social relationships is minimised and the opportunities to build on social success while continuing to work on social understanding and problem-solving maximised. It is also helpful to try to elicit the perspective of the child with PDA about why they have taken a dislike to another pupil. There are occasions when potential conflict can be reduced by making small adjustments such as altering the seating arrangements, changing group activities and reducing other potential stressors in sessions with that pupil (e.g. making changes to the sensory environment, or putting the pupils together in a more motivating lesson rather than a more difficult subject).

Demonstrating empathy and social consequences may be supported by using visual approaches such as flow charts like Figure 7.3.

Although it is important to be working towards developing empathy in children with PDA, it may be necessary to motivate initial changes in behaviour by highlighting better outcomes for the child with PDA. This should of course run alongside more in-depth work on their developing emotional understanding and social conscience.

The example in Figure 7.3 was created for and with Joshua following discussion in his mentoring sessions with his teacher Mrs Webb. Joshua had been finding it difficult to tolerate another pupil in his class. Class staff had reduced the time they were together and were moving forwards with a plan for them to be together only for some of Joshua's preferred lessons.

Figure 7.3 describes a scenario when asking the child with PDA to be more considerate would not be sufficient to bring about a change in their behaviour. It is not intended to be presented as an alternative to promoting empathy, but as additional to doing so. It is intended that more considerate behaviour will emerge from an initial degree of self-interest, allowing time for social understanding and impulse regulation to develop.

The example may represent where the work begins but it is not where it ends. In the meantime, we are providing a means of working through social problem-solving that leads to a better outcome for Sophie and for Joshua. Sometimes we need a pragmatic starting point for managing everyday classroom situations. Furthermore, the process of completing a flow chart like this one may identify important areas to be included elsewhere in PSHE work and in Personal Tutorials. It may also be helpful to link it to other ways of demonstrating consequences as well as predicting (and thereby avoiding) overload. These may include activities such as giving a child a number of boxes to carry simultaneously, each one representing a task or potential stressor or irritant in order to demonstrate capacity and overload: in difficult moments, which box should we decide to put down for a while? It could also be reinforced, for example, by keeping a diary or photo album of positive social and emotional problem-solving or interactions.

It's annoying that I have to work in a group with Sophie on Tuesday mornings

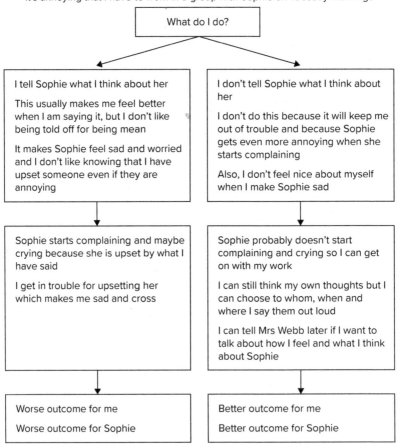

| What do I do? |
|---|

| I tell Sophie what I think about her | I don't tell Sophie what I think about her |
|---|---|
| This usually makes me feel better when I am saying it, but I don't like being told off for being mean | I don't do this because it will keep me out of trouble and because Sophie gets even more annoying when she starts complaining |
| It makes Sophie feel sad and worried and I don't like knowing that I have upset someone even if they are annoying | Also, I don't feel nice about myself when I make Sophie sad |

| Sophie starts complaining and maybe crying because she is upset by what I have said | Sophie probably doesn't start complaining and crying so I can get on with my work |
|---|---|
| I get in trouble for upsetting her which makes me sad and cross | I can still think my own thoughts but I can choose to whom, when and where I say them out loud |
| | I can tell Mrs Webb later if I want to talk about how I feel and what I think about Sophie |

| Worse outcome for me | Better outcome for me |
|---|---|
| Worse outcome for Sophie | Better outcome for Sophie |

*Figure 7.3 Joshua and Sophie*

If a child with PDA develops a dislike that is focused on a member of staff we will need to consider a different response. Again, the teaching points remain as above. Interacting with an adult is hopefully easier to manage because of the adult's own maturity and professional responses but some members of staff can be left feeling unfairly targeted. This is something that we will come back to in Chapter 9 when we think about how to look after yourself. In terms of school organisation, if a member of staff is on the receiving end of a negative focus it may be wise to reconsider how much time that adult spends with the child. It may be beneficial to reduce their contact at least for a time, during which time they are given a different emphasis in their role with the pupil, such as working with them on a more motivating or fun activity. Alternatively, there may be a particular interest or skill that the adult has which could be something they can share with the child with PDA, such as baking or playing a musical instrument.

## Promoting emotional wellbeing

When describing the principles underpinning Collaborative Approaches to Learning in Chapter 3, we emphasised the need to be proactive and to foster emotional resilience and self-reliance. This section will now discuss these themes in more detail. Our own experience has shown us that for children with a PDA profile there often seems to be a sense of fragility and a lack of permanence in their learning. When things are going well, and the environment and the way they are approached and managed is sensitive and responsive, we tend to see a reduction in anxiety and the child's need to be in control. This, in turn, enables them to be more tolerant of other people and their expectations. Unsurprisingly, these periods tend to be ones during which there is greater engagement, learning and progress. We need, though, to be careful of not becoming complacent. We should think carefully about how much of this is dependent on us 'getting it right' at the moment and how much is due to a more fundamental and long-lasting change 'within the child'. Looking to the future we need to be sure that we are doing as much as we can to help the child become equipped to better regulate their emotions and manage situations for themselves, so that they are not quite so dependent on other people always 'getting it right' for them. Over time this should become a responsibility shared between the adults and the pupil.

It can be easy for those working with children with PDA to focus on the characteristics of the child that stand out and seem to directly impact on them, the adults. For example, challenges may be presented in the way in which the child avoids their expectations and requests, how they can be controlling of other pupils, or the lack of depth in their empathy for other people. For the child themselves though, their experiences are often characterised by anxiety, feeling unsafe, a fear of or sense of failure and low self-esteem. Over time, this can erode their emotional wellbeing and have a negative impact on their feelings of self-worth and their mental health.

In 2010 the National Autistic Society published a document called *You Need to Know* investigating the impact of mental health problems on children with ASD and their families. The report referred to findings that 71 per cent of children with autism develop mental health problems (such as anxiety or depression) compared to a prevalence rate of around 10 per cent in other children. In the same year the final report of the national review of the Child and Adolescent Mental Health Services (CAMHS; DCSF/DoH 2010) was published and emphasised the role that all professionals have to play in promoting mental health, stating in its foreword that 'we all play a part in helping children and young people grow up. Mental health and psychological well-being are not the preserve of one profession or another, or of one government department or another.' The report went on to point out that 'Schools...play a pivotal role in promotion, prevention and early detection of emotional well-being and mental health issues, bringing in other professionals as appropriate' (p.3).

This has been reflected in the increasing emphasis in educational policy and practice on promoting emotional wellbeing in all children. This has included *Every Child Matters* (DfES 2004), *Social and Emotional Aspects of Learning* (DCSF 2007), the Ofsted framework (2018) and the *Special Educational Needs and Disability Code of Practice* (DfE/DoH 2015). Indeed, children's mental health has never had a higher profile than it does now, and in autumn 2017 the *Child and Family Clinical Psychology Review* (Faulconbridge *et al.* 2017, p.2) made a recommendation that 'the development of psychologically healthy schools which support the wellbeing of staff and students should be a priority for all'. The publication also made a specific reference to the challenges that children with neurodevelopmental difficulties present in school due to problems with staff and peer relationships and went on to talk of the need to 'develop positive strategies to help children cope and other children to understand them' (p.2).

We have considered various ways to personalise the curriculum of a pupil with PDA. Before we go into more detail let's first think about some of the themes that may guide both our *teaching* and the pupil's *learning* in this area.

There is considerable current discussion in education about how to promote emotional resilience in ourselves and in the youngsters we support. Doing so requires reflecting on a number of issues. When we work with younger children, we try to provide a supportive environment so that their emotional wellbeing is protected and so that we reduce occasions when they are tipped into overload. As these pupils mature we need to move towards fostering in them more strategies that they can understand and begin to use independently. This is where the notion of resilience comes in. In recognition of the fact that we cannot protect children from all stress, upset and disappointment that everyday life brings, we have an important role to play in helping them gain the capacity to recover when one of these difficulties affects them. Some children may be stressed by big challenges such as moving house or schools, others may find it hard to manage if, for example, a preferred member of staff is absent, leaving them too anxious that day to access a usually enjoyable lesson. Depending on the extent or intensity of the stress, upset or disappointment some children may need more time or more help to recover on some occasions than others. We will need to personalise a set of learning intentions and devise strategies to support this process. The most effective approaches are able to support a child on their most straightforward day and on their toughest day.

Understanding their own emotions is likely to be challenging for pupils with PDA and a helpful starting place might be for pupils to be able to recognise the physical signs of distress. This could include recognising a faster heartbeat, sweating, nausea, restlessness, increased self-soothing habits. It can be useful to encourage children with PDA to recognise what is 'usual for them' and therefore what is outside *their* ordinary. Learning to respond by using calming techniques, which could include deep breathing or squeezing a stress ball, when children realise that some of these feelings are happening can be helpful not only in calming them but thereby giving them more processing time.

It is important to remember that a child's problem-solving skills, use of language and communication, ability to predict outcomes and impulse control will be compromised at times of raised anxiety. There also may be a general mismatch between the chronological, emotional, social and academic 'age' of a child with PDA to be taken into account. Equally we should take time to encourage young people to look after some of the physiological elements of wellbeing such as having a healthy diet, a good sleep pattern, staying hydrated, regular exercise and so on.

We have mentioned that it can be helpful for the adults supporting children with PDA to delay or defer difficult decisions to give themselves more thinking or liaising time, and the same is true for young people too. It is probably true for most of us that we don't make our best decisions when impulsive, under pressure or anxious. Children with PDA are no different in this respect and it is a useful skill as they mature to be able to identify a complicated decision and put it off until they can find out more information, have time to process it or are able to talk it through, for example at home or in a Personal Tutorial.

### Recognising the context of promoting emotional wellbeing

Throughout this book is the repeating theme that PDA is character-ised by anxiety. It is this anxiety that drives the avoidance. Naiha (aged 14) said:

> For me, feeling anxious is normal. It's just a question of *how* anxious I am rather than *if* I am anxious.

Many factors in a child's life can add to this anxiety, including even attending school and engaging with their education once they are there. When we lower a child's anxiety we don't only strengthen their emotional wellbeing but we also increase the chances of their participation and therefore improve their learning opportunities.

In this section we will set out some day-to-day considerations necessary to support a pupil's emotional wellbeing.

To give us some context about an individual child we need to:

### Understand the pupil's perspective

Be creative, patient and observant in how we determine a child's views. We can use a variety of indirect approaches to encourage them to communicate their thoughts. These might include using puppets or role play. It might be possible to use a character that the child already knows from a book, especially one with a persona that demonstrates emotions clearly, such as the Mr Men series, X Men, Dr Who or Harry Potter characters. It may be helpful to use techniques that provide a visual framework to discuss choices, views and emotions. It is also important to ensure that you collaborate with the other adults who live or work with the pupil and include views and responses that might have emerged in a range of contexts or outside school. Providing the time and space for this kind of work in schools is something that will be covered in the section on Personal Tutorials later in this chapter.

### Recognise the expectations involved in going to school

There are many demands that are implicit in the everyday routines of a typical school day. Not every pupil with PDA will be sensitive to all of these but as school staff we should be aware of the school experience for our pupils. The list of these expectations is potentially long when we reflect on how often we expect pupils to arrive at a precise time, line up, sit in a predesignated seat in class, wear uniform, organise equipment, complete work tasks, have food and breaks according to a timetable and so on. On the one hand, there are some aspects of routine that are really important in providing structure and reducing uncertainty for pupils with PDA. On the other hand, it is likely, given the number of implicit demands in schools, that a pupil with PDA will be sensitive to a proportion of them. If we think of a pupil's tolerance like a teacup with a finite capacity, we need to take care not to overfill the cup with the less important expectations so that we leave enough space for priority learning and behaviour. To stick with this analogy, you will be able to safely contain even less tea in the cup on a day that the cup has to be carried across a muddy field balanced on a saucer.

### Promote personal regulation

Children with PDA will benefit from activities that keep them regulated in their emotions, in their engagement and in their sensory systems. Activities that can provide these will need to be individualised. It helps to base tasks on special interests and to include an element of physical activity. In some cases, input from an occupational therapist who can advise regarding a sensory programme provides useful guidance. Activities which promote relaxation and engagement need to match the preferences and interests of the particular pupil. It is really important that assumptions are not made about what would suit or motivate a child, for example regarding genres of music or choice of sport. When children are younger the adults supporting them have a greater role in providing regulating activities and a calming environment. As children mature we want them to improve their self-awareness so that they know what works for them and can apply these strategies for themselves.

### Promote emotional understanding and problem-solving

Children with PDA will need to develop an understanding of their own emotions and the emotions of other people, and then work towards how they can use this knowledge to manage their emotional wellbeing. Initial steps are to identify their emotions, maybe by simply naming and categorising emotions. Some children respond well to devising their own personal 'dictionary' of emotional vocabulary that they understand. This can be made fun by adding exaggerated photographic examples. Children will also need to understand the emotions of other people, including how to look out for indicators of emotion in people they know, then to make sense of what is likely to have contributed to them. This learning can be demonstrated by using drawing, role play or games such as Jenga (where you remove blocks from a tower until it topples). Working out what will soothe them if they are becoming unregulated or anxious is important. This could involve a few trials of various techniques which the child then grades and matches to different levels of effectiveness; for example, reading a favourite comic was good for what one child described as 'imagination boredom' but was not effective for 'leg boredom', which was better suited to running around the field.

Developing skills to improve and repair their social relationships as they mature will help them into the future. Supporting them to understand their strengths and difficulties will improve their self-awareness and inform them to make wise choices and take balanced risks as adults.

**Keep emergency exits clear**

The need to be flexible, to allow processing time and to provide regulating activities has been discussed many times. We know that children with PDA can be changeable. This means that in order to adapt to this changeability we too need to keep our options open. On occasion that may require having an 'emergency exit' available. In practice it might be you having a standby activity based on a personal interest 'up your sleeve' if it becomes necessary. It might mean that on a school trip you take a staff car as well as the coach so that there is the option of quieter travel or even an earlier/later departure time. If a child is variable in relation to what they will eat of school meals, you might keep a stock of 'emergency rations' to use on a day they have not been able to have lunch.

## *Creating designated time to focus on promoting emotional wellbeing*

Developing emotional resilience in pupils with PDA requires additional time and support. It requires time to work with the child and also time to support the adults delivering this role. It is always going to be more effective if our approach to developing resilience is done proactively rather than in response to a crisis. This is not only because this helps to avoid moments of crisis arising in the first place, but also because preventing flashpoints is a much better use of staff time than dealing with the consequences of not having been able to avert them. Therefore there needs to be a commitment by senior leaders as well as by classroom practitioners to protecting time to work on this area of learning. It is also important to set aside time for discussion and guidance for school staff working directly with the pupil.

We have previously described a system called 'Personal Tutorials' for meeting the emotional wellbeing needs of pupils (Christie *et al.* 2008; Christie *et al.* 2012). Personal Tutorials are individualised one-to-one sessions between a pupil and their tutor which provide dedicated time to focus on social and emotional learning. Tutors can be classroom staff or may have another role within school. Tutors should themselves receive training, support and supervision in their work. It is recommended that Personal Tutorials happen regularly (such as once a week) so that a predictable forum to work on emotional wellbeing is embedded in a pupil's timetable. Issues covered in tutorials should be decided collaboratively between family and professionals and there should be frequent opportunities to review progress and priorities.

The starting point for Personal Tutorials is making time to build a positive relationship with a pupil. This is mentioned in Chapter 5, where we talk about getting to know the child and understanding their perspective. Building rapport is not a quick process. However, it represents an invaluable investment of time in promoting the wellbeing, learning and co-operation of pupils with PDA. Although it may be helpful to have some input from specialist professionals, school staff should recognise the unique opportunities they have to build relationships with their pupils. Being able to get to know a child over time and at a pace that suits them is important. Knowing their classmates and their family and being with them so often that you can choose your moment to address a tough issue are huge advantages. The positive impact everyday staff working in schools can make should not be underestimated.

If you have other specialists or therapists involved such as autism outreach services, speech and language therapists or CAMHS, you will need to ensure that you maintain clear communication and key messages between all involved, working closely with families too.

## Delivering Personal Tutorials
### Personal Tutorials: Content
There are two aspects of the content of Personal Tutorials. The first is regarding the style of the sessions and the second is regarding the identified areas for learning.

In relation to the first of these it will be useful for you to refer to the strategies detailed in Chapter 4, since these will guide you to develop a style that is characterised by flexibility, indirect demands, the use of humour and novelty and personal interests. When it comes to adapting these approaches to promoting emotional wellbeing, this is where it can be helpful to have introduced the system of any tool you want to use before you add the element of emotional content. For example, if you want to use a visual grading chart to determine how a child feels about various aspects of their school day, it is wise to have already used this system to grade something much less emotionally 'charged', such as foods or films. You may also find it helpful to use visual ways of demonstrating a range of feelings, which can be made more meaningful if you incorporate a child's own expressions or vocabulary.

Work with Ben in this respect began with drawing up his personalised scoring grades which was initially applied to films he had seen, as in Figure 7.4.

| Film | Score | Grade |
|------|-------|-------|
| Fast and Furious 5 | 10 | Totally Sick |
| Harry Potter 2 | 9 | Awesome |
| Fast + Furious 3 | 8 | Really Cool |
| Despicable Me | 7 | Epic |
| Moana | 6 | Cool |
| Wallace + Gromit | 5 | Pretty good |
| Inkheart | 4 | Not bad |
| Harry Potter 5 | 3 | Rubbish |
| Diary of a Wimpy Kid | 2 | Don't Bother |
| Frozen | 1 | Waste of space |
| A cheesy Romance | 0 | Just No! |

*Figure 7.4 Oscar nominees*

Ben then went on to complete another table based on a discussion about various aspects of the school day. A further column was later added to this format to incorporate emotions linked to these experiences, as shown in Figure 7.5.

| Part of School Day | Score | Grade | Usual Feelings About This |
|---|---|---|---|
| Art and Free time | 10 | Totally Sick | Absorbed and Excited |
| Minecraft Club | 9 | Awesome | Inspired and fun |
| Outdoor PE | 8 | Really Cool | Good Fun |
| ICT | 7 | Epic | Happy and Interested |
| Science + Maths | 6 | Cool | Interested |
| Indoor PE | 5 | Pretty Good | Medium Fun |
| Dinner time | 4 | Not Bad | Hungry |
| Literacy | 3 | Rubbish | Irritated and Fed up |
| Tests e.g. Spelling | 2 | Don't Bother | Annoyed and Nervous |
| Assembly | 1 | Waste of Time | Bored and Fidgety |
| Getting Ready in the morning | 0 | Just No | Annoyed and Worried |

*Figure 7.5 School life*

In developing a system of Personal Tutorials, we felt that it was crucial to remain focused on the individual and fluctuating needs of each pupil. In our practice, we chose to describe the aims of Personal Tutorials as 'areas of focus' rather than as targets, in order to identify issues to work on in a sufficiently flexible way that remained responsive to each pupil's pace and priorities.

Emma enjoyed her tutorial and had a good relationship with her tutor but recognised that she didn't feel comfortable with too much pressure. She commented:

> I want to be able to talk to you about feelings but that's my hardest subject. It's best for me if we do something else while we have a chat, like cooking, building with K'nex or colouring.

Deciding the areas of focus is done in collaboration with a range of staff involved, with the family and with input from the pupil themselves. Areas of focus also reflect the particular current circumstances that affect a child within and outside the classroom. In respect of *how* to deliver the areas of focus we refer you to the full range of strategies outlined in Chapter 4. The key to successful Personal Tutorials is building trust and rapport, especially in the early stages, which is achieved gradually and often via personal interests. What works particularly well is using activities that offer opportunities for choice, and are indirect and fun.

One pupil said of his sessions:

> Tutorials are my best lesson of the week... It's a time when what I think matters...they make me feel important...everyone should have one.

Some areas of focus that have featured in Personal Tutorials for pupils with PDA have included:

- to recognise physical sensations associated with increased anxiety and implement previously rehearsed techniques to reduce stress, for example: *Use the list previously worked on, e.g. raised heartbeat, sweating, dry mouth, and add any further details. Practise familiar relaxation techniques (blowing a feather, deep pressure, mindful fingertip counting)*

- to learn to use visual grading systems to score preferences, beginning with everyday choices such as favourite food or TV shows and working towards more complex issues such as subject choices, for example: *Use visual charts to develop a five-point system to grade food/TV shows 'best to worst'. Keep the learning confined to setting up the system at this stage. Moving forwards this can be extended to grade social and emotional experiences*

- to plan a trip to the cinema, researching variables and incorporating a Plan B option, for example: *Choose a film to see at Cinemax in town and plan the trip. This will include planning the journey, costing travel, ticket price and snacks. Contingency planning to cover a 'Plan B' choice of film, bus and snack should the initial plan be unavailable for any reason*

- to role play typical playground situations using puppets to test various social alternatives and consequences, for example: *Within general imaginative play with hand puppets include themes of games often played in the playground. Issues to explore include asking to join a game, coming to an agreement about altering the game, turning down a particular game and suggesting an alternative*

- to prepare a contribution to their person-centred plan by dictating their views or creating a filmed 'interview', building on their interest in filmmaking and interviewing and being interviewed, for example: *Frame the interview using the guidelines of pupil contribution to the review process. Questions to be worded in an individualised way and shown to them in advance. Den room to be used for filming and additional filming sessions booked in case a number of 'takes' are required*

- to discuss and make choices regarding travel, activities and menu for end of term school trip, for example: *Explore map and activities on offer at the water sports centre. Go with member of staff on pre-visit to walk around the venue. Make a choice between travelling on school minibus or in member of staff car (doesn't need confirming until the day of the trip). Make a first and second choice of activities at the water sports centre (this will have to be confirmed three days before the trip). Plan packed lunch which can be bought the day before trip and can include baking done at school.*

Personal Tutorials are not intended to be implemented in isolation from other curriculum opportunities. They should be seen within the framework of PSHE, social communication and independence skills.

Although they are distinct sessions within a pupil's timetable, the work around them is planned and delivered and progress is recorded as part of their broader individualised curriculum. They provide a forum to explore issues and teaching points as much as they are a place to develop self-management techniques and independence skills, which will have benefits beyond a pupil's experience of school.

Talking in a tutorial about her meltdowns Yasmin reflected:

My meltdowns feel like there's a fire inside and I don't know what to do with it. I can't think straight and I don't care about anything or anyone else when I get that upset. I feel like my emotions are too big and too wild to stay inside so they have to break out. Afterwards I can feel shocked about what has just happened. And I feel really exhausted. It makes such a difference to be with people who look after me afterwards instead of people who shout at me because of what I've done. I can't think about that until later... Meltdowns used to happen to me a lot when I was younger. Now I'm 16 I can cope a bit better.

## Promoting self-awareness

A key component of emotional resilience lies in developing self-awareness. For any of us, the more conscious we are of our own strengths as well as our weaknesses, the more balanced our expectations will be of ourselves. We all benefit from developing an understanding of what helps us and what hinders us, what soothes us and what stresses us and of how far to push ourselves so that we grow without forcing ourselves beyond what is wise or healthy for us as an individual. This is a lifelong learning project but as we get more skilled at it we will be more likely to experience positive relationships, emotional wellbeing and meaningful work opportunities. These are also aspirations we have for the young people with PDA who we support. Facilitating this learning fits well into Personal Tutorials and may include elements of the areas for development shown in Table 7.1, which could form the basis for identifying areas of focus.

**Table 7.1 Areas for personal development**

| Area for development | May include aspects of: |
|---|---|
| Recognising own preferences | • Beginning with neutral topics such as TV programmes or food types, identify personal preferences and note how these differ from those of other people<br>• Move onto grading other areas such as subject learning, personal interests, activities |
| Express choices and understand consequences of choices made | • Understand making a choice between two or more options<br>• Predict outcomes of choices made in terms of practical, social, organisational and emotional consequences |

*cont.*

| Area for development | May include aspects of: |
|---|---|
| Develop an understanding of own strengths and weaknesses | • Physical and academic strengths<br>• Areas needing more support, e.g. wearing glasses to see the whiteboard, needing more processing time<br>• Compare different strengths and weaknesses in individuals, e.g. compare various attributes and preferences of pupil and tutor<br>• Begin to consider what personal areas of strength could lead to in respect of skill improvement or employment opportunities |
| Recognising what helps and what hinders | • Develop awareness of the individualised benefits of e.g. movement breaks, working in a quiet area, having a scribe, etc.<br>• Recognise what hinders, e.g. in terms of the sensory environment, impact of lack of sleep or of hunger, being distracted by a stressor or worry<br>• How can we maximise situations where there is access to what helps and minimise situations of exposure to stress? |
| Understanding difficult situations retrospectively | • Consider alternative problem-solving strategies that could have been preferable and may be useful another time<br>• Recognise what happened that helped and didn't help the situation<br>• Understand their impact on the situation and whether any social repair is necessary<br>• Consider whether and how to have another attempt at this task |
| Develop an understanding of their condition and how it affects individuals | • Understand 'my form of autism' and the implications, the strengths it enhances as well as some of the challenges it may bring<br>• Recognise that there are different ways people they know are affected by their form of autism<br>• Recognise when and to whom it would be advisable to talk about their form of autism |

The areas and the aspects outlined in Table 7.1 are very broad in order to illustrate the range of points that could be covered. It would not be recommended that you work on all aspects of each of these areas simultaneously but prioritise and pace them according to individual need.

In relation to the work you may do with young people regarding supporting them to understand their own form of autism and the implications of it, this work needs to be considered extremely carefully. It has been described more fully in our previous book (Christie *et al.* 2012). Carrying out this work should be discussed in detail with a child's family or carers before undertaking and should include agreed resources, key messages and regular follow up. Publications describing a condition from the perspective of a child, such as *Can I tell you about PDA?* (Fidler and Christie 2015) may be useful to support these conversations.

### Personal Tutorials: Organisation

If you think it would be helpful to put a system of Personal Tutorials in place for a pupil or a number of pupils, you will need to consider:

- **Choosing a member of staff who is going to be a good match with this pupil:** Which member of staff has a positive relationship with the child? Do they have any particular skills or hobbies that could engage the pupil? Can they reliably be made available within the organisation of the school staffing structure?

- **Which is the best location and timetable slot of the day to use for a Personal Tutorial?** Where do you have a quiet space available? Does it suit the pupil's sensory sensitivities if there are any issues in this respect? Which is a good part of the day for them to be engaged and receptive? Could you put their tutorial as an alternative to a lesson that is not working well for them at the moment? How long should the sessions be at this stage?

- **How will you maximise pupil participation and encourage pupils to express their views in these sessions?** How can Personal Tutorials be tailored around their interests? What approaches are known to encourage participation? Which techniques can be used to help them express their views, for example indirect visual strategies?

- **How will you build in time to liaise with other adults?** What is the plan to protect time to feed back significant developments to classroom staff, family and senior staff?

- **Decide which areas of the child's wellbeing to prioritise:** Who needs to be involved in collaboration regarding identifying areas of focus? How will you include the views of the pupil?

- **How will you address the areas of focus?** What activities will be used to work on the areas of focus? How should you present them, for example, through which interests or activities?

- **How will you monitor, assess and report on progress?** Who will be involved in evaluating progress towards identified areas of focus? How will this progress be moderated and reported to the child, family and other staff? How will the way you report progress in social and emotional learning fit in with other school systems of assessment?

- **How will you support development of staff skills and supervise practice?** Who will take the lead in supervising this work? How will time be made to debrief with staff on a regular basis and to oversee next steps in staff practice?

Making sessions positive for the child will provide opportunities to cover meaningful topics and allow complex themes to unfold. In the long term, sessions like these might provide insight into problems from the pupil's perspective, and enable them to reflect on their experiences and work with you to develop strategies to regulate their emotions and behaviour.

As his self-awareness improved during Personal Tutorial discussions George began to realise:

> I like to have choices but not too many choices. Especially if I'm stressed, having too many choices can be too much to think about... I like to have choices set out on a piece of paper that I can go away and think about before making a decision.

Tutorials are not only a time for pupils to access an important part of their curriculum, but also a time for the adult to learn more about the pupil they support. Our aim in these sessions is to gain a better understanding of what makes sense to this child and to build rapport, and what we learn will help us come up with strategies that will be effective for each child as an individual.

## Personal Tutorials: Recording

Child-centred flexible sessions are not always straightforward to record and monitor. It is important that as part of a robust system within an educational setting Personal Tutorials are subject to thorough recording, monitoring and assessing. Determining what is of sufficient note to track can be done in discussion with colleagues and may lead to a tutorial being logged as in Table 7.2.

**Table 7.2 Tutorial recording sheet for Maggie and Vivianne**

| Pupil and tutor | Maggie and Vivianne |
|---|---|
| Date and length of session | 12 June, 50 mins |
| Area(s) of focus | • To test a variety of relaxation techniques over the term<br>• To develop Maggie's use of visual systems of grading her views |
| Activities/features during session | • Foot spa with lavender oil<br>• Variety of music genres<br>• Visual chart used to grade how relaxing the different genres of music listened to were |
| Significant occurrences | Maggie was motivated and co-operative throughout today's session. She didn't try to postpone the start of the tutorial by checking on the fish or tidying the noticeboard as previous weeks. She was particularly keen that we both completed charts to grade our own different preferences of the music genres we listen to. She was open to the idea of putting together a personalised relaxation playlist. |
| Themes to follow up | Maggie said that she liked music with 'heavier' drum beats and she liked to match her breathing to a given number of beats. She wondered whether her heart rate could sync with music she likes.<br><br>Maggie said she had heard about mindful chocolate eating and wants to try this another week. |

*cont.*

| Links to other learning | • Liaise with music teacher about exploring other music apps or other percussion instruments that could be used to 'pace' breathing |
| | • Overlap with PSHE group re emotional literacy |
| Information passed on from this session to: | Parents, class teacher, music specialist (Mum and Dad have mentioned looking into a Saturday music club she could join). |

A downloadable blank version of this chart is available in the Appendix.

## Evaluating effectiveness of Personal Tutorials

It is difficult to evaluate effectiveness of the work done in Personal Tutorials because it is not done in isolation, that is, it happens alongside a range of other learning such as PSHE curriculum, social opportunities and naturally occuring maturity. It does not fit easily into conventional ways of measuring progress in schools, which is a theme that is described further in Chapter 8. This is where additional or 'soft' data has a key role to play. That might mean that as a child's wellbeing improves we see improvement in other areas of their school experience such as increased attendance, longer periods of concentration, more engagement in learning and fewer incidents of difficult behaviour. Progress may also be reflected in comments that staff, pupils and their families make which all represent a valuable contribution. For instance, staff have commented:

'Working in this way has freed me up to concentrate on building relationships with pupils in my class.'

'Personal Tutorials have opened the door to more interaction, co-operation and therefore also learning both within the sessions and back in the classroom.'

Parents' comments have included:

'I know how much his tutorials mean to him because if he is ever off ill on a tutorial day he asks to be taken into school so he doesn't miss that part of the day.'

And pupils have added:

> 'I knew it was important to come to school the day after my hamster died, even if I was late, because I needed to talk about it.'

> 'I wouldn't be bothered if I even had to miss playtime, I'd rather have more tutorial time than playtime. It's my favourite lesson. I don't know why I love tutorials, I just do!'

One pupil, who is also referred to in our previous publication (Christie *et al.* 2012), reflected on his Personal Tutorials and drew the picture in Figure 7.6 to illustrate the flow of conversation in his sessions, saying:

> ...our time together is useful and it's interesting...things are better for me...I used to think I was the one who should change. I don't think that now. Now I know it's OK just to be me.

*Figure 7.6 Banter*

# Chapter 8

# DEMONSTRATING PROGRESS

## Counting what counts

As with any pupil, when planning a curriculum for a young person with PDA, it is necessary to ensure that appropriate arrangements are in place for assessing and recording progress towards identified outcomes. Ensuring an accurate picture of both attainment and progress can, however, be challenging, for a range of reasons. Factors such as levels of anxiety, sensory needs, relationships with staff and peers and motivational issues can all have an impact on a pupil, resulting in a varied or uneven picture of performance. Traditional assessment processes such as tests or exams may be particularly difficult for a child with PDA since they present with explicit demands and staff will need to be aware of this when deciding on the most appropriate assessment systems to use. This may involve using more indirect approaches in order to assess knowledge and skills, for example, missions and challenges, projects, quizzes, practical tasks.

Important to this process is clarity about the purpose of assessments being carried out and the function of the information they provide. *Summative assessment* provides information on what a child has learned at the end of a given period and on how effective the teaching has been in supporting the child to achieve the desired outcomes. In Chapter 6 on personalising the curriculum we described an example of this type of assessment for a child with PDA (Arron) in relation to a unit of work on literacy. As well as indicating what the child has achieved, this format allows for comments on *how* this learning took place by including examples and also highlighting where adult support has facilitated this achievement.

In addition to its summative function, you may also use *formative assessment*, whereby information is provided that informs planning and next steps. Teachers will carry out this type of assessment both formally and informally on an ongoing basis. In Chapter 7 a framework was suggested for supporting staff to record key elements of Personal Tutorials (Table 7.2). This included the recording of significant occurrences which were then used to inform next steps for future sessions. There was also an emphasis on discussion with others working with the child in order to plan ways forward. The value of this type of qualitative data should not be underestimated since it provides practitioners with important information about both the child and the effectiveness of teaching strategies in achieving desired outcomes. It also provides evidence of progress in areas of need specific to individual children, such as emotional wellbeing or sensory needs. Other ways in which this information can be gained include parental contributions and feedback from the children and young people themselves, such as the comments below:

> 'The work done in Personal Tutorials to help my son accommodate his sensory needs has benefitted my whole family.'

> 'Personal tutorial sessions are an essential part of my boys' development. Without emotional wellbeing it's more difficult to achieve any progress.'

> 'Even if you're at your most depressed emotion, tutorials always help you feel better. Solving problems in your life is easier when you talk about it. It helps to rebuild your confidence after a difficult time.'

Another example of using assessment information both summatively and formatively can be seen in the example below. The extract is from a teacher's summative assessment for a child with PDA, following a unit of work based on a popular children's book. As can be seen, the assessment provides information about what the child has achieved but is also useful in identifying ways forward in relation to successful teaching strategies and areas for development. Features related to the child's PDA, and ways in which the child is being supported to accommodate these, are apparent within the text.

> Emily is very enthusiastic about Literacy as a subject. She often comes with her own ideas for what the lesson should be about but accepts that there is other work to be done and has contributed very well to the sessions...

Emily is able to read silently but as a result will often read ahead rather than following the reader during group reading. She has a wide vocabulary and was able to suggest a range of adjectives to describe characters...

Emily relies on her phonic knowledge to spell words, which can lead to inaccuracies. She has generally accepted help with her spelling although on occasion has insisted that it is 'my way' of spelling it. The use of a 'spell checker' has been effective in helping Emily to make the corrections needed...

When asked to write creatively she often has her own agenda and needs to be persuaded to do the prescribed task. She generally is able to complete the task but is often in a rush to get it done and her written work in this context does not always reflect her imaginative capabilities. It was interesting that when a member of staff scribed for her when asked to write an alternative version of a nursery rhyme her work was far more adventurous and showed a good understanding of what was expected.

As can be seen, strategies such as using a spell checker and scribing ideas have been effective in supporting Emily to engage with sessions and make progress in her learning in ways that take into account her PDA. The assessment provides useful information for planning future priorities and ways in which learning should be supported.

Although schools will have systems for tracking progress related to the National Curriculum and qualifications, it is important to recognise that outcomes in a range of other areas are likely to need to be prioritised for young people with PDA. In the example above, for example, although the literacy learning is described in detail, what is not so apparent to those who may not know the child well is the progress that has been made in areas that may fall outside the National Curriculum. These may include the child's social and emotional development or their ability to tolerate sensory input. For a child with PDA, making progress in these areas may be essential to their ability to engage with learning in academic subjects.

Changes to the National Curriculum and a move away from assessment linked to levels in 2014 (DfE 2014) have highlighted the need for a broader approach to assessment, particularly for pupils with special educational needs and disabilities (SEND). The Commission on Assessment without Levels in its 2015 report makes specific reference to the need to measure progress for pupils with SEND across a range of areas:

> Schools should consider meaningful ways of measuring all aspects of progress including communication, social skills, physical development and independence. Assessment should reflect the extent to which a pupil can apply their learning in a wider range of contexts and enable teachers to determine what they need to do to ensure that the intervention and support provided enable children to progress in all areas of their learning and development. (DfE/STA [Standards and Testing Agency] 2015)

Since the advent of assessment without levels, schools have been reviewing their assessment systems with an awareness that 'one size does not fit all' and that a range of different tools may be required in order to provide a rounded picture of achievement for each pupil. In keeping with the idea of a personalised curriculum is the concept of schools having a range or basket of indicators which reflect different aspects of a child's achievement and progress and allow these to be celebrated. Also important is ensuring that assessment is not an end in itself but part of a cycle of planning, intervention review and assessment (Figure 8.1) as advocated by the Special Educational Needs and Disability Code of Practice (DfE/DoH 2015): the 'graduated approach'.

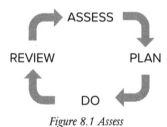

*Figure 8.1 Assess*

The Rochford Review (STA 2016), although primarily concerned with assessment arrangements relating to primary English and mathematics for pupils working below age-related expectations, was welcome in its acknowledgement of a number of issues pertaining to children and young people with SEND. These included:

- reference to the existence of an uneven profile, whereby children's ability in relation to different areas may vary considerably

- the need for schools to choose a curriculum that meets the needs of their pupils and to align assessments with this curriculum

- the need to tailor assessment to individual needs and unique profiles

- parents' wish for their child to make progress in relation to their individual needs.

Also of relevance to children with PDA was an emphasis in the Rochford Review on engagement as a precursor to subject-specific learning, based on the work of Barry Carpenter for the Complex Learning Difficulties and Disabilities (CLDD) project (Carpenter 2015). The Engagement for Learning Framework (E4L/SSAT 2011) includes an Engagement Profile (Figure 8.2) and Scale and the Engagement Ladder, which can be used to explore and identify effective teaching and learning strategies for children with complex needs and provide evidence of progress towards engagement. The seven areas of engagement identified are: initiation, responsiveness, curiosity, investigation, discovery, anticipation and persistence. For some pupils with PDA, such a framework can provide a useful structure for focusing in on effective prerequisites for learning.

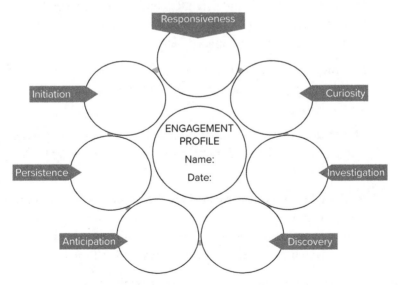

*Figure 8.2 Engagement Profile*
Adapted from CLDD Research Project Resources © Crown Copyright 2011

## Areas of need: Demonstrating progression

Schools are responsible for choosing and formulating their own assessment processes and it is important to have a range of indicators for different aspects of a child's development. A tool developed specifically for measuring progress for children and young people on the autism spectrum is the Autism Education Trust's Schools Autism Progression Framework (AET 2016). With funding from the Department for Education the Progression Framework was drawn up in 2016 following consultation with schools and other education services, parents, and young people and adults on the autism spectrum. It focuses on areas of learning, set out below, that fall outside the National Curriculum but which may be priority areas of need for a child with autism.

### AET Progression Framework areas of learning

**Social communication** – expressive communication, listening and understanding, conversations

**Social interaction** – being with others, positive relationships (with adults), friendships (with peers), group activities

**Sensory processing** – understanding and expressing own sensory needs, responding to interventions, increasing tolerance of sensory input, managing own sensory needs

**Learning** – organisation and independent learning, motivation and engagement, school routines and expectations, evaluating own learning

**Independence and community participation** – independent living, road safety and travel, personal safety, keeping healthy, personal care, leisure

**Emotional understanding and self-awareness** – understanding and expressing own emotions, managing emotions and behaviour, understanding other's emotions and intentions, self-awareness, developing confidence and self-esteem.

As well as allowing school staff to track a pupil's progress in these areas, the Framework also supports an understanding of the individual profile of each child. Each area is broken down into a series of learning intentions which supports staff in understanding needs and in identifying next steps. An extract from the *managing emotions and behaviour* section provides an illustration in Table 8.1.

**Table 8.1 Extract from AET Progression Framework: Managing Emotions and Behaviour**

| 2. Managing emotions and behaviour | |
|---|---|
| Learning to regulate and control their emotions will allow pupils to have increased access to a range of experiences and environments. Although it is vital that staff provide support in this area the aim should be for pupils to work towards an increasing level of independence so that they are able to understand and manage their own needs in this area in a range of contexts. | |
| Links: Understanding and expressing own emotions, Managing own sensory needs | |
| **Learning intention** | **Notes** |
| 2.1 Responds to calming strategies of others | |
| Accepts and responds positively to calming/comforting strategies of others | Adult understands and has strategies that work well for the young person, e.g. squeezes, singing |
| Seeks comfort from others when distressed or anxious | |
| 2.2 Uses own strategies to manage stress | |
| Is able to comfort self/self-soothe when experiencing mild distress | E.g. using a comfort object |
| Uses own strategies to self-regulate/ distract self | E.g. using behavior such as humming, spinning, rocking |
| 2.3 Uses taught strategies to manage emotions and behavior | |
| Participates in identifying strategies to help self-regulate | E.g. using a stress release object, taking self to a safe place, time with special interest |
| Participates in adapting environment/ taking preventative action to help themselves self-regulate | E.g. putting on ear defenders as noise level rises |
| Practices self-regulation strategies during calm periods | E.g. when regulated |
| Uses planned/taught/agreed strategies to self-regulate | E.g. follows visual cue to take a break, takes time out with preferred activity |
| Evaluates effectiveness of self-regulation strategies | |
| Uses different self-regulation strategies according to context/venue | E.g. has a 'hidden' fidget object for assembly |

A key feature of the tool is its emphasis on identifying priorities which are individual to a young person. So for a young person with PDA the emphasis when setting priorities may be on managing emotions and behaviour (*emotional understanding and self-awareness* section) or on motivation and engagement (*learning* section). For example, for Grace (whose personalised curriculum was described in Chapter 6) priorities might focus on supporting her to manage her own emotions and regulate her behaviour as well as to increase her engagement with the curriculum. Learning intentions for Grace drawn from the AET Progression Framework might therefore be as follows:

---

## Learning intentions drawn from AET Progression Framework – Grace

### Managing emotions and behaviour

- Participates in identifying strategies to help self-regulate
- Identifies stress signals and uses planned strategies

### Motivation and engagement

- Engages in series of negotiated tasks in a sequence chosen by them

### School routines and expectations

- Follows agreed strategy for movement or 'overload' break away from classroom

### Managing own sensory needs

- Reflects on response to sensory sensitivities and suggests adaptations/interventions for future use

---

The Progression Framework supports the planning of personalised programmes by identifying key areas of learning and allows progress to be recorded. It can be used to support the drawing up of outcomes and targets for statutory documentation such as Education, Health and

Care Plans (EHCPs) (DfE/DoH, 2015) and for school SEND planning such as Individual Education Plans (IEPs) or Pastoral Support Plans (PSPs). As part of this process it is important to ensure that the views of the young person are included. Personal Tutorials may provide a useful forum for this type of work, allowing the young person to have a voice about their aspirations and providing an opportunity for reflection using a range of strategies as described in the section on Personal Tutorials in Chapter 7. The views of parents should also be sought, both in their own right but also to ascertain whether the young person expresses the same views at home and at school and to triangulate different viewpoints.

Once learning intentions have been identified, a baseline assessment is made so that progress from the starting point can be tracked at agreed points throughout the year. This information is useful for sharing with parents and other professionals involved in the pupil's education and can be supported by evidence showing how the pupil has achieved the learning intentions. Since more conventional forms of evidence (e.g. written work) may not be available, staff will need to be creative in collecting material that supports their judgements on a pupil's achievements. Evidence might include written accounts (e.g. of discussions within lessons), Post-it® notes highlighting a significant event that demonstrates what the pupil can do, or evidence of direct contribution using alternatives to writing (e.g. drawings, computer-generated material, scribed notes).

To conclude this chapter, it might be useful to consider the following, alongside the personalised curriculum checklist at the end of Chapter 6 (Table 6.4):

- How will we use assessment to inform our planning?

- What kind of evidence will support our judgements?

- How well are our systems set up to report progress to families and to the pupils themselves?

# Chapter 9

# LOOKING AFTER YOURSELF

Earlier parts of this book have outlined some principles and strategies for supporting the learning of pupils with PDA. This chapter will focus on the support and wellbeing needs of the adults who are working with them. This is not to minimise the support needs of families but reflects the focus of this book being on education professionals.

We will look at some of the common issues affecting adults and suggest a variety of useful strategies for school staff to adapt to their setting.

Working with children with PDA can be rewarding but can also be very intense. That's usually because you are supporting a child who is unpredictable and who is often highly anxious. Even when you are working positively with a pupil you will need to use a proportion of your own energy to navigate their variable emotions, to plan creatively and to think on your feet. This is all very tiring. You will also need the energy to manage your own emotions especially on days when the pupil is particularly anxious and avoidant or when you are under more pressure.

As we have said, teaching and learning is a two-way transactional process. If we are to be most effective at working with this group of children who can be hard to engage we need to take account of our own resilience. As well as being professionals, we are also people who have our own needs and differences. This is an area that is all too often overlooked in some schools and organisations.

## What are common issues for school staff?

Having worked with a variety of staff in a range of settings, we have observed some commonly reported themes in the experiences of adults working with pupils with PDA.

One teacher commented:

> I've worked with children with autism for 15 years and I thought I did a pretty good job of it. In some ways, this pupil has been similar to the others, but at the same time significantly different from them. It's confusing. The usual strategies haven't worked and I am left feeling de-skilled and utterly worn out... We need to develop a different approach now.

Staff often talk about feeling:

- **confused**: It is hard to understand why this child on the autism spectrum does not respond well to the usual 'autism-friendly' strategies.

- **frustrated**: Staff have tried many different approaches, some of which work some of the time. It is hard to predict when they will work and hard to sustain progress even when they do.

- **isolated**: Adults may have found it necessary to work in a different way to other colleagues in the school and sometimes feel misunderstood or judged for using adapted teaching techniques.

- **de-skilled**: Sometimes they begin to question their skills or experience because previously successful methods used with other pupils are not working for this child.

- **stressed and exhausted**: The unpredictability of the child and the quick thinking required of the adult supporting them can be draining. Some staff also find it anxiety provoking to spend extended periods of time with another person who is anxious and who has mood swings. This group of pupils can be very intense to work with, which is tiring. Some classroom staff would like more support from their managers than they receive.

- **demoralised**: Adults feel downhearted if a period of positive participation is followed by a significant dip in engagement. It makes it hard to feel they are building on success or previous progress.

- **under pressure**: Adults feel that they can't show any 'chinks in their armour' even if they are under par for any reason because they feel the child will use this 'weakness' to their advantage. They may also feel under pressure about the progress they want to help the child make. It can be especially frustrating if a child is achieving below their academic potential or doesn't seem to be fulfilling the expectations that other people have for them. Balancing the needs of a pupil with PDA with those of the others in a class can also be a pressure on staff.

- **criticised**: Sometimes children with PDA will overstep social boundaries and make personal remarks. Some adults find it more difficult than others not to take this to heart. That can be especially the case if the criticisms are personal or if they happen to hit a nerve. Reminding ourselves that pupils are most likely to criticise us when they are feeling highly anxious and therefore defensive can help us find a positive way to respond.

- **concerned about the pupil's wellbeing and long-term future**: Staff talk about feeling concerned about the future prospects and wellbeing of a child. This is particularly the case if staff become aware that a child's learning is not as secure as they thought it was, for instance, if they move classes or department and don't seem to have retained skills. It can leave the adults worrying about long-term success. It is also a common concern that children who are highly anxious may have significant difficulties in the long term regarding their mental health.

- **concern about supporting families**: The families of many of these pupils understandably need additional support. This can have an effect on school staff not only in terms of liaison time needed but also because their genuine empathy for a family has an emotional impact on them too.

Clearly these are strong and at times difficult emotions and families also experience some of these feelings in bringing up their children with PDA. Of course, they won't apply to all of you all of the time and there are many positive responses to working with pupils with PDA which we will also cover.

## How can schools support their staff?

Each school is different but if a school is going to be effective it needs to promote and ensure a positive ethos with highly motivated and well-supported staff. This is reflected in the Ofsted common inspection framework, which states that in making judgements on the effectiveness of leadership and management inspectors will consider (amongst other criteria):

- how well leaders ensure that the school has a *motivated, respected and effective teaching staff* to deliver a high quality education for all pupils, and how effectively governors hold them to account for this

- the quality of *continuing professional development for teachers* at the start and middle of their careers and later, including to develop leadership capacity. (Ofsted 2018, p.43)

It is not feasible to provide detailed solutions to specific school settings. However, we will outline some of the key points of good practice which can be adapted to various situations.

### Having time to talk

Having time to talk to others who can support your setting is important. This includes staff working at all levels and involves managers who are in a position to make accommodations in classrooms or within the timetable. It might mean talking to other people who also know the child and can offer feedback on making sense of a behaviour or situation. It might include other colleagues within your school or local networks who recognise the challenges you face. Try to focus on understanding other people's perspectives, not on being critical. It is a very commonly reported problem in schools that there is not enough time to do much more than grab a conversation in passing. There is no quick fix to this but remind yourselves how much time you will have to find to resolve a difficult situation if you have not managed to talk in order to prevent it developing into an issue. Schools can consider the structure of staff meetings, how often these happen and how advice or supervision is woven into these discussions. There is also scope for focused work within systems of performance management and continuing professional development.

## *Providing space to reflect*

Behaviour and engagement can be changeable in pupils with PDA. This in turn means that we need to be responsive in how we interpret and react to the pupils we support. It is not always straightforward to get the balance right between sticking with a plan long enough to allow it time to work and deciding when to change our approach. Doing this wisely requires time to reflect and discuss. Schools are busy environments and we recognise this is easier said than done. However, protecting regular time slots to plan, discuss and reflect will actually promote more supportive and effective ways of working together and can ultimately save time by avoiding a difficulty escalating.

In our experience, supporting reflective practice in staff discussion can be helped by posing some of the questions in Table 9.1. (A downloadable version is available in the Appendix.) It is important that we ask these questions of ourselves without blame or judgement but in the spirit of learning from recent events so that we can work towards ongoing improvements.

Table 9.1 Reflective practice questions

| Pupil .................................... Staff .................................... | Date ............ Action points fed into.................. ................................................ ................................................ Staff informed .......................... ................................................ |
|---|---|
| What did I do well? Do I know why these successful strategies worked well? How can I use some of them again in the future? | |
| Did I stand by the expectations I asked of him/her? If not, why not? Did I abandon them or postpone/adjust? If yes, were they realistic and reasonable? Were they non-negotiables? | |

*cont.*

| | |
|---|---|
| Did I overreact? <br><br> If so why? <br><br> Did that reflect pressures I am under and what are these? <br><br> Can I access more support or advice? <br><br> Was my reaction impacted upon by additional factors, e.g. other pupils? <br><br> Environmental risks? | |
| What have I done to support keeping him/her regulated? <br><br> Changes to the environment? <br><br> Using personal interests? <br><br> Sensory adaptations? <br><br> Offering opportunities for choice? | |
| If asked in the right way can he/she tell me more about why that went particularly well or badly for him/her? <br><br> How can I best have this conversation with him/her? <br><br> What can I do with the feedback he/she provides? | |
| Did I get the balance right between encouragement and directness? <br><br> What did I do to encourage? <br><br> What did I do to instruct? <br><br> What has this demonstrated to me about working with this pupil? | |
| Are there any other strategies I wish I had tried? <br><br> If so, what are they? <br><br> What prevented me from using them on this occasion? <br><br> How can I increase the chances of using them in the future? <br><br> If not, would it help to think about developing some different strategies? | |

| | |
|---|---|
| Have I repaired (as necessary) and continued to reinforce my positive relationship with him/her?<br><br>What approaches did I use to do this?<br><br>What have I done to facilitate repair following a difficult incident? | |
| What else do I want to log that I have learned recently that is important to share with my colleagues?<br><br>Where should I log these thoughts?<br><br>Who should I inform?<br><br>How can these thoughts feed into revising our approaches, systems, timetable, staffings, etc.? | |

Some settings view having complex pupils as an opportunity to forward their school development. They may set up a focus group or working party to extend and embed good practice. These may be in house or might include other colleagues in local networks. Schools who do this put themselves at a real advantage, not only in meeting the needs of a particular pupil but in furthering their expertise, in valuing their staff and ultimately in being in a better position to respond to other pupils.

### Rotating core staff

Early on, you will probably have a small number of staff who work with a pupil with PDA. As time goes on it is wise to extend this core team so that there are sufficient members of staff to rotate. This makes allowance for the occasions when staff are unwell or attending training as well as giving adults natural breaks in the intensity of their role. Over time, extending the team of staff who work with a pupil will also prevent the child from becoming dependent on only a few key people. Having a range of staff who work well with a pupil with PDA can also be a good strategy for defusing potential conflict. If you find yourself in a situation where you have reached something of a stalemate with a child, you can often 'shift the mood' and get their engagement back on track by temporarily changing the adult supporting them.

## Accessing specialist training and guidance

Accessing specialist training on PDA will promote a better understanding of the condition as well as provide guidance on recommended strategies. It is not always possible to resource this in every setting but helpful information about supporting pupils with PDA can be sourced, such as that available via the PDA Society website (www.pdasociety.org.uk). It is obviously important that, where training is accessed, key members of staff working directly with the pupil attend as well as managers. It is also important that other members of staff who will come across pupils with PDA have a general awareness of the condition and the implications of accommodating these pupils at your school. For instance, it can be helpful if other classroom staff have guidance to understand why there may be altered boundaries or priorities for a particular pupil. Office staff and lunchtime supervisors will benefit from some of this knowledge too. Decisions and plans should be communicated to all staff. It is equally important that senior leaders are fully aware of the challenges and pressures their staff may encounter.

It will contribute to a more successful and sustainable educational placement if you can access guidance regarding planning an appropriate curriculum, managing difficult behaviour, supporting transitions, working with other professionals and liaising with families. Sometimes senior leaders within a school can provide this, drawing on guidance from advisory teams which can then be embedded into school practice.

## Maintaining clear leadership and responsibiities

As with other children with complex needs, there can be a sizeable team that supports a pupil with PDA. This team includes a range of adults who work with a child in school as well as their family and other professionals who may be involved. Throughout this book is an emphasis on collaboration and this needs to be co-ordinated. Schools play a pivotal role in bringing these teams together since they usually have the most day-to-day contact with a child other than their families. It works well to have a nominated lead professional and clearly designated responsibilities. For instance, maybe the headteacher or SENCO takes the lead role in drawing together other professional input, co-ordinating meetings and making decisions. It could be the pastoral lead or specialist teaching assistant who takes responsibility for everyday liaison with the family.

## Observing and guiding each other supportively

Children with PDA can present differently in different situations and with different people. Try not to take it personally if you are finding a pupil hard to engage at the moment and try not to take it for granted if you are having success. These dynamics may change over time in both directions. Instead make good use of opportunities to observe and learn from each other. Support positive and honest discussions about different perspectives. During an observation of a typically successful session take note of the environment, the social demands of the situation, the language and style of interaction the member of staff uses, the processing time offered, and the balance of choice and expectation. Note also how the member of staff responds if the child has completed the task successfully as well as how they respond if the child has avoided or rejected the task. Take time to reflect on and discuss these observations with colleagues.

## Building on good relationships and key strengths of staff

Once you have built a core number of positive relationships with a pupil with PDA you have a really good base from which to promote all sorts of learning opportunities. We all have different strengths and interests and we can use these assets to encourage participation. For instance, if a pupil develops an interest in a subject it can be helpful to link them to a member of staff who can personalise their learning. You may have a member of staff who breeds dogs, who has an allotment, who plays in a band or who repairs vintage motorbikes. These skills could be inspirational to some pupils. Plus, many children with PDA respond well to feeling that they are being taught by an 'expert'. It can also be rewarding and valuing to the adults to present activities through an interest of their own. The pupil may then 'coach' another child or adult through their new learning, offering them opportunities for social interaction while revising new knowledge. For example, a child with PDA with an interest in textiles may teach another child or adult how to use a sewing machine so that they can produce handmade Christmas cards to sell as part of their mini-enterprise project.

### Being aware of burnout and retaining equilibrium

As we have already mentioned, children with PDA require a high degree of stamina in the adults who support them. This should be recognised by education practitioners and their managers so that they can support each other and act preventatively if they see signals of burnout in a colleague.

As a practitioner, recognise when something has happened that has troubled you. Try to understand why this has occurred and look at what can be done to resolve the situation and avoid it happening again. Make sure you also take time to do something that helps you regroup. Good managers recognise that this is an important factor in staff being able to do their job well today, and tomorrow. During the working day it might be as straightforward as making small amendments to staff timetables such as providing additional breaks or preparation time. Breaks help staff to gather their thoughts and offer extra preparation time which may be necessary to personalise lesson content or to provide alternative work. It is important that we achieve a balance between working intensively with complex pupils alongside maintaining the wellbeing and ultimately the attendance and retention of valued members of staff.

## What are the most positive features of supporting pupils with PDA?

Pupils with PDA may certainly be amongst the most challenging children we might work with but they may also be some of the most rewarding. They may stretch us in our attitudes and our preconceptions. This can be good for us as practitioners and as people. They can teach us about humility, flexibility, resilience, collaboration and priorities. We should be encouraged to view being led out of our familiar comfort zone as an opportunity for growth.

Some positive outcomes that staff have reflected on after working with a pupil with PDA include:

- **presenting work tasks**: 'I am less rushed in my responses to a certain set of circumstances or a behaviour. I have learned to take a moment to think about what if I do it like this…what if I don't do it like this…what if I address it later…what if we do it together…what if we take it somewhere else…'

- **confidence**: 'I have been in some rather challenging situations and we have worked our way through them. That's not easy but it helps me feel stronger and more capable than if I had not been "tested".'

- **decision making**: 'It feels more natural now to take my time before I make a decision and to use that time to discuss with others involved. Sometimes the pupil themselves comes up with a reasonable solution if given time, other times they move on to the next thing anyway.'

- **closer relationships**: 'I have been able to build a closer relationship with him and his family by having had to take extra care to understand what makes him tick. That is not only rewarding but is really helpful in managing any future situations.'

- **being creative**: 'Finding flexible and creative ways to teach her has been really enjoyable. Not all my ideas have been successful but it has been liberating to be able to take a teaching point and think of personalised fun ways to explore it together.'

- **having fun**: 'Sharing a good sense of humour and using this to create rapport. Engaging any pupil is rewarding. Finding a way to engage a pupil who is really difficult to engage is especially rewarding.'

- **being flexible**: 'Remembering that it will help everyone if our options can be kept open. This means not making assumptions about how a child will respond. It means offering choices that will suit us as well as the child. It means remembering that there will always be another way to achieve the same end.'

In summary, a key element to a successful educational placement for a pupil with PDA is that it is sustainable. This requires careful management not only of the engagement and wellbeing of the child but also of the adults who support them.

Staff teams who can use creative approaches in their teaching style, curriculum and boundary setting and who can do so in a way that supports each other as well as the child and their family are most likely to be successful. Settings that protect time for staff to liaise, to observe each other and to access guidance will have staff who are better equipped to work collaboratively and positively. Educational settings where there is an ethos of understanding, not of judgement, will promote commitment and motivation in the people who work there.

# SUMMARY

## A FINAL WORD

Over the previous chapters we have described the needs of a group of children who have distinctive and complex difficulties in social understanding, communication and behaviour. Typically this group of children have very high levels of anxiety and find it hard to tolerate the demands and expectations of other people. They are also often adept at avoiding these 'perceived demands' and can be controlling of other people and aspects of their environment. This profile has been described as pathological demand avoidance. We have set out the developments in our understanding of how this profile is dimensional, varying in its extent and nature and best understood as being part of the autism spectrum.

Furthering our understanding of children who share this pattern of development and behaviour has important implications for those who live and work with them. They seem to need more flexibility and negotiation, and a less direct style than is typically the case with other children on the autism spectrum. We have described the style and approach that seems best suited to their needs as Collaborative Approaches to Learning. At the heart of the approach is recognising the transactional nature of teaching and learning and the need for the adult to modify their style, and be more flexible, responsive and accommodating. You need to adapt your expectations according to the pupil's mood and level of tolerance as we depicted in Figure 2.1 in Chapter 2 showing the two dials.

Our experience of working with many families, schools and staff in education settings has shown that some people find adopting this stance easier than others. The capacity to do this might be influenced by their own beliefs, attitudes and experience. It may well also be determined by the amount of support available to them, or the organisational constraints and barriers that might exist in the setting in which they work. The need for schools to be flexible and responsive has been stressed earlier, as have some of the ways in which staff can be supported to work most effectively and maintain their own resilience.

Another theme that we have emphasised throughout the book has been the need to prioritise the personal and social curriculum and strive to promote emotional resilience and wellbeing. There is little known about the issues that face children with PDA as they move into adulthood and what factors influence how well they adapt to this transition. There has, though, been more work carried out in connection with individuals on the autism spectrum more generally. In 2011 Karin Wittemeyer and her research team published a report on behalf of the Autism Education Trust looking at 'educational provision and outcomes for people on the autism spectrum'. This report strongly questioned whether educational planning for children with autism is directed towards reaching good outcomes in adulthood. Amongst the key outcomes that were identified as being most important by individuals with autism and their families were the following: meaningful employment, good social relationships (underpinned by self-confidence and good self-esteem), independent living and good mental health (including being less anxious).

In the Introduction we noted that, early on, the clinical descriptions and other accounts of PDA had been very cogent and resonated with parents and teachers alike. There was, though, a need to underpin this with more of a research base. We briefly outlined some of the developments that have taken place over the last few years. Inevitably these have focused on trying to better recognise the profile and how it fits within diagnostic terminology and classification systems, so that there is more consistency in the way that it is described and understood. There is now a need to broaden the research focus to encompass work looking in more detail at ways in which children with PDA can best be supported. Research on educational interventions is a complicated area because of the number of variables that can influence an individual's life and their progress. In the field of autism research all the comparative evaluations of different interventions suggest that some children do well with one form of intervention and others do not (Jones *et al.* 2008). At the same time consensus has been reached that there is an evidence base suggesting that certain elements are crucial components of any approach. Some of these (e.g. close involvement of parents and carers and a focus on social understanding and communication) are equally applicable to children with a PDA profile. Others, such as the degree of structure used and the amount of choice offered, require a different emphasis in our experience.

The need for this change in emphasis has been reinforced in the limited research to date, such as the report produced by the Centre for Research in Education (Brede *et al.* 2016) and the accounts by Gore Langton and Syson (n.d.) referred to in Chapter 2. It would seem timely for this sort of study to include a larger number of pupils and a range of different settings.

Perhaps the main motivation for us in developing Collaborative Approaches to Learning has been the recognition that more conventional strategies were seldom effective for children with a PDA profile. We were coming across many children, families and schools where behavioural approaches and structured teaching methods had been advocated but were proving to be too confrontational and were often worsening the situation. The outcomes were typically raised anxiety levels, increased avoidance and breakdown of school placements. The O'Nions *et al.* (2016a) paper that we referred to in Chapter 1, endorsed this when noting the findings of Gore Langton and Frederickson (2015) that individuals displaying this PDA profile were frequently being excluded, often 'even from specialist schools'. When the 'Education and Handling Guidelines', the precursors to Collaborative Approaches to Learning, were put in place we were finding that difficult incidents were reduced and children seemed to become calmer and more accessible to learning. This picture was reinforced as we developed our own provision for pupils with PDA within a specialist setting and has continued to be the case in our work supporting a wide range of schools through training, or in an advisory and consultancy role for individual pupils.

A pupil whose views were being sought in the process of educational planning reflected to us:

> Actually, there aren't loads of changes the school have made but they have made a big difference. Even though the teachers still decide what I do it's better for me to have some choices about when to do my work and whether to do it in the classroom or in the library.

A headteacher, following a piece of consultation work, talked about how reframing their understanding of a pupil's profile and modifying the strategies that they used had made an enormous difference.

> We have such a better understanding of what makes her tick now...using different strategies has made the world of difference to school staff, to her family and most of all to Sasha herself. It's amazing how big an impact making small changes in emphasis and priorities can make. Her mum describes it as nothing short of transformational for their home life! At school, we are so much better equipped to move forwards with a more flexible and positive education for Sasha.

A SENCO in another primary school wrote to us some months after work around assessment of a pupil and whole school training to update us on progress.

> The support and advice was a real help and we're sure that without it we wouldn't be celebrating the successes we are today.
>
> Yesterday was Josh's leaver's assembly and performance, he was a true star. He performed a scene with the help of two of his friends and his parents were both there and so proud of him and couldn't believe how far we have come. Josh was also really proud of himself and enjoyed sharing the assembly with his family. He has become a very happy, confident young man, with a developing emotional understanding which helps him to overcome moments of anxiety.

# Appendix

Table 4.1a Priority rating chart

| Pupil name:<br>Class, age: | | |
|---|---|---|
| How important is it that s/he... | Priority level | Comments, rationale and plan |
| | | |
| | | |
| | | |
| | | |
| | | |
| Completed in consultation with: | Date: | Next review of the above planned for: |

Autism
Associates

## Table 4.3a Adaptation to task

| Class/group: | Date: |
|---|---|
| Task as planned by class teacher for the group | Task adapted for |
|  |  |
| Follow-up work for the group | Follow-up work for |
|  |  |

## Table 4.8a Flexible visual schedule

| Today is ........................................................ | | |
|---|---|---|
| These are the choices today | | |
| ................................... will be in class to help you today | | |
| Please decide a timetable together with ............................................. | | |
| **Lesson 1** | **Lesson 2** | **Lesson 3** |
| | | |
| **Breaktime:**<br>Choose: | **Lunchtime activities:**<br>Choose: | **Home time jobs:** |
| | | |
| **Free time choices for another day:** | **Work to finish another day:** | **Reminders:** |
| | | |

### Table 4.11a Maximising participation prompt sheet

| THIS IS THE TASK... |  |
| --- | --- |
| (this may be an everyday task, a piece of work, a new activity, etc.) | |
| **How can I increase participation by considering...?** | |
| What adaptations can I make to the environment? | |
| What adaptations can I make to the group? The seating plan? | |
| How would it be helpful for me to introduce the task? | |
| Is this task an agreed priority? | |
| What motivators would be helpful? | |
| How should we deploy the staff available? | |
| How can I adjust the expectations? (not only by reducing them) | |
| What opportunities for choice can I offer? | |
| What opportunities can I offer for building on the pupil's strengths or interests? | |
| How will it be helpful to respond if the task goes well? | |
| How will it be helpful to respond if the task does not go well? | |

The learner is offered:

- Choice (what, when, how, where)
- Personal interests
- Support from trusted adult(s)
- Individual learning style

| **What?** | **Curriculum areas covered** |
| --- | --- |
|  |  |

Staff provide:

- Facilitated learning
- Various recording methods
- Guided support towards success
- Background work to support the timetable and curriculum

| **How?** | **When/Where?** |
| --- | --- |
|  |  |

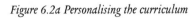

*Figure 6.2a Personalising the curriculum*

## Table 6.4a Personalised curriculum checklist

| | |
|---|---|
| Have we identified learning priorities?<br><br>How have we done this?<br><br>Who has contributed to the discussion? (e.g. young person, parents) | |
| Do the activities within the young person's timetable provide opportunities to address these learning priorities? | |
| Does the timetable take into account barriers to learning for this pupil?<br><br>Have we made sufficient adaptations to expectations?<br><br>Environment?<br><br>School rules/systems?<br><br>Who is co-ordinating the timetable?<br><br>Have decisions about adaptations been approved by those co-ordinating/overseeing the curriculum? | |
| How are opportunities for engagement maximised?<br><br>Are we using opportunities for personal interests?<br><br>Are teaching methods engaging?<br><br>Are we offering opportunities for extending or offering new interests? | |

| | |
|---|---|
| Who is involved in supporting the child? <br><br> Who is their trusted adult? <br><br> Which peers do they identify as their friends? | |
| Do we have sufficient resources to make a personalised curriculum work? <br><br> Space? <br><br> Staffing? <br><br> Materials? <br><br> Subject knowledge? | |
| Have we set learning outcomes that we can measure? (i.e. academic and non-academic areas) <br><br> How will we demonstrate progress? <br><br> What kind of evidence will support our judgements? <br><br> How will we use this information to inform our planning? | |

Autism
Associates

## Table 7.2a Tutorial recording sheet

| Pupil and tutor | |
|---|---|
| **Date and length of session** | |
| Area(s) of focus | |
| Activities/ features during session | |
| Significant occurences | |
| Themes to follow up | |
| Links to other learning | |
| Information passed on from this session to: | |

Autism
Associates

## Table 9.1a Reflective practice questions

| Pupil .......................................... <br><br> Staff ...................................... | Date ............ <br> Action points fed into the following documents................. <br> ............................................... <br> ............................................... <br> Staff informed .......................... <br> ............................................... |
|---|---|
| What did I do well? <br><br> Do I know why these successful strategies worked well? <br><br> How can I use some of them again in the future? | |
| Did I stand by the expectations I asked of him/her? <br><br> If not, why not? <br><br> Did I abandon them or postpone/adjust? <br><br> If yes, were they realistic and reasonable? <br><br> Were they non-negotiables? | |
| Did I overreact? <br><br> If so why? <br><br> Did that reflect pressures I am under and what are these? <br><br> Can I access more support or advice? <br><br> Was my reaction impacted upon by additional factors, e.g. other pupils? <br><br> Environmental risks? | |
| What have I done to support keeping him/her regulated? <br><br> Changes to the environment? <br><br> Using personal interests? <br><br> Sensory adaptations? <br><br> Offering opportunities for choice? | |

Autism
Associates

| | |
|---|---|
| If asked in the right way can he/she tell me more about why that went particularly well or badly for them?<br><br>How can I best have this conversation with him/her?<br><br>What can I do with the feedback he/she provides? | |
| Did I get the balance right between encouragement and directness?<br><br>What did I do to encourage?<br><br>What did I do to instruct?<br><br>What has this demonstrated to me about working with this pupil? | |
| Are there any other strategies I wish I had tried?<br><br>If so, what are they?<br><br>What prevented me from using them on this occasion?<br><br>How can I increase the chances of using them in the future?<br><br>If not, would it help to think about developing some different strategies? | |
| Have I repaired (as necessary) and continued to reinforce my positive relationship with him/her?<br><br>What approaches did I use to do this?<br><br>What have I done to facilitate repair following a difficult incident? | |
| What else do I want to log that I have learned recently that is important to share with my colleagues?<br><br>Where should I log these thoughts?<br><br>Who should I inform?<br><br>How can these thoughts feed into revising our approaches, systems, timetable, staffings, etc.? | |

# References

## Introduction

APPGA (2017) *Autism and Education in England 2017: A Report by the All Party Parliamentary Group on Autism on How the Education System in England Works for Children and Young People on the Autism Spectrum.* London: National Autistic Society.

## Chapter 1

American Psychiatric Association (1994) *Diagnosis and Statistical Manual of Mental Disorders,* 4th edn (DSM IV). Washington, DC: APA.

Christie, P. (2007) 'The distinctive clinical and educational needs of children with pathological demand avoidance syndrome: Guidelines for good practice.' *Good Autism Practice 8,* 1, 3–11.

Christie, P., Duncan, M., Fidler, R. and Healy, Z. (2012) *Understanding Pathological Demand Avoidance in Children: A Guide for Parents, Teachers and Other Professionals.* London: Jessica Kingsley Publishers.

Jones, G., Baker, L., English, A., Lacey, P., Lyn-Cook, L. and Robertson, C. (2012) *AET National Autism Standards.* London: Autism Education Trust.

NAS (n.d.) *What Is Pathological Demand Avoidance (PDA)?* Accessed on 01/05/2018 at www.autism.org.uk/PDA.

National Initiative for Autism (2003) 'National Autism Plan for Children.' *The National Autistic Society.*

National Institute for Health and Clinical Excellence (2011) *Autism Spectrum Disorders in Under 19s: Recognition, Referral and Diagnosis.* London: NICE.

Newson, E. (1998) in collaboration with Christie, P. and staff of Sutherland House School. *Education and Handling Guidelines for Children with Pathological Demand Avoidance Syndrome.* Ravenshead, Nottingham: Information Service, Elizabeth Newson Centre.

Newson, E., Le Marechal, K. and David, C. (2003) 'Pathological demand avoidance syndrome: A necessary distinction within the pervasive developmental disorders.' *Archives of Disease in Childhood 88,* 595–600.

O'Nions, E., Christie, P., Gould, J., Viding, E. and Happé, F. (2014) 'Development of the Extreme Demand Avoidance Questionnaire (EDA-Q): Preliminary observations on a trait measure for pathological demand avoidance.' *Journal of Child Psychology and Psychiatry 55,* 758–768.

O'Nions, E., Happé, F. and Viding, E. (2016a) 'Extreme/"Pathological" demand avoidance.' *British Psychological Society DECP Debate,* issue 160, i–v.

O'Nions, E., Gould, J., Christie, P., Gillberg, C., Viding, E. and Happé, F. (2016b) 'Identifying features of "Pathological Demand Avoidance" using the Diagnostic Interview for Social and Communication Disorders ('DISCO').' *European Child and Adolescent Psychiatry 25*, 407–19.

Sherwin, J. (2015) *Pathological Demand Avoidance Syndrome: My Daughter Is Not Naughty.* London: Jessica Kingsley Publishers.

Wing, L., Leekam, S., Libby, S., Gould, J. and Larcombe, M. (2002) 'Diagnostic interview for social and communication disorders: Background, inter-rater reliability and clinical use.' *Journal of Child Psychology and Psychiatry 43*, 307–325.

World Health Organization (1992) *The Tenth Revision of the International Classification of Diseases and Related Health Problems* (ICD-10). Geneva: WHO.

## Chapter 2

Brede, J., Remington, A., Kenny, L., Warren, K. and Pellicano, L. (2016) *Back to School: Paving the Path to Re-integration for Autistic Children Previously Excluded from Education.* London: National Autistic Society.

Gore Langton, E. and Syson, Z. (n.d.) *Simple Strategies for Supporting Children with Pathological Demand Avoidance at School.* Accessed on 19/04/2018 at www.pdasociety.org.uk/resources/education-resources/educational-strategies-booklet-from-positive-pda-2.

## Chapter 3

Christie, P. (2007) 'The distinctive clinical and educational needs of children with pathological demand avoidance syndrome: Guidelines for good practice.' *Good Autism Practice 8*, 1, 3–11.

Christie, P., Duncan, M., Fidler, R. and Healy, Z. (2012) *Understanding Pathological Demand Avoidance in Children: A Guide for Parents, Teachers and Other Professionals.* London: Jessica Kingsley Publishers.

Newson, E. (1998) in collaboration with Christie, P. and staff of Sutherland House School. *Education and Handling Guidelines for Children with Pathological Demand Avoidance Syndrome.* Ravenshead, Nottingham: Information Service, Elizabeth Newson Centre.

## Chapter 6

Christie, P., Duncan, M., Fidler, R. and Healy, Z. (2012) *Understanding Pathological Demand Avoidance in Children: A Guide for Parents, Teachers and Other Professionals.* London: Jessica Kingsley Publishers.

DfE/DoH (2015) *Special Educational Needs and Disability Code of Practice: 0 to 25 Years: Statutory Guidance for Organisations Who Work with and Support Children and Young People with Special Educational Needs and Disabilities.* London: DfE/DoH.

DfE (2018) *Preparing for Adulthood.* Accessed on 06/08/2018 at https://www.preparingforadulthood.org.uk/

Hartley, D. (2009) 'Personalisation: The nostalgic revival of child-centred education.' *Journal of Education Policy 24*, 4, 423–434.

Pellicano, L. (2014) 'A future made together: New directions in the ethics of autism research.' *Journal of Research in Special Educational Needs 14*, 3, 192–218.

Public Health England (2015) *Promoting Children and Young People's Emotional Health and Wellbeing.* London: PHE.

Walliams, D. (2011) *Billionaire Boy.* London: HarperCollins.

Wittemeyer, K., Charman, T., Cusak, J., Guldberg, K., *et al.* (2011) *Educational Provision and Outcomes for People on the Autism Spectrum: Executive Summary.* London: Autism Education Trust.

## Chapter 7

Christie, P., Duncan, M., Fidler, R. and Healy, Z. (2012) *Understanding Pathological Demand Avoidance in Children: A Guide for Parents, Teachers and Other Professionals.* London: Jessica Kingsley Publishers.

Christie, P., Fidler, R., Butterfield, B. and Davies, K. (2008) 'Promoting social and emotional development in children with autism: One school's approach.' *Good Autism Practice 9,* 2, 32–38.

DCSF (2007) *Social and Emotional Aspects of Learning.* London: DCSF.

DCSF/DoH (2010) *Children and Young People in Mind: The Final Report of the National CAMHS Review.* London: DCSF and DoH.

DfE/DoH (2015) *Special Educational Needs and Disability Code of Practice: 0 to 25 Years: Statutory Guidance for Organisations Who Work with and Support Children and Young People with Special Educational Needs and Disabilities.* London: DfE/DoH.

DFES (2004) *Every Child Matters.* Nottingham: DFES.

Faulconbridge, J., Hickey, J., Jeffs, G., McConnellogue, D., *et al.* (2017) 'What good looks like in psychological services for schools and colleges: Primary prevention, early intervention and mental health provision.' *Child & Family Clinical Psychology Review, 5.*

Fidler, R. and Christie, P. (2015) *Can I tell you about Pathological Demand Avoidance Syndrome? A Guide for Friends, Family and Professionals.* London: Jessica Kingsley Publishers.

NAS (2010) *You Need to Know.* Campaign. Accessed on 19/04/2018 at www.autism.org.uk/get-involved/campaign/successes/you-need-to-know.aspx.

Ofsted (2018) *School Inspection Handbook.* Manchester: Ofsted. Accessed on 14/06/2018 at https://assets.publishing.service.gov.uk/government/uploads/system/uploads/attachment_data/file/699810/School_inspection_handbook_section_5.pdf.

## Chapter 8

AET (2016) *Schools Autism Progression Framework.* Accessed on 19/04/2018 at www.aettraininghubs.org.uk/schools/pf/.

Carpenter, B. (2015) *Engaging Learners with Complex Learning Difficulties and Disabilities.* London: Routledge.

DfE (2014) *National Curriculum and Assessment from September 2014: Information for Schools.* London: DfE.

DfE/DoH (2015) *Special Educational Needs and Disability Code of Practice: 0 to 25 Years: Statutory Guidance for Organisations Who Work with and Support Children and Young People with Special Educational Needs and Disabilities.* London: DfE/DoH.

DfE/STA (2015) *Final Report of the Commission on Assessment without Levels.* London: DfE/STA.

E4L/SSAT (2011) *The Engagement for Learning Framework Guide.* Accessed on 19/04/2018 at www.engagement4learning.com/wp-content/uploads/2017/01/Engagement-for-Learning-Framework-guide-2.1.16.pdf.

STA (2016) *The Rochford Review: Final Report.* London: STA.

## Chapter 9

Ofsted (2018) *School Inspection Handbook.* Manchester: Ofsted. Accessed on 14/06/2018 at https://assets.publishing.service.gov.uk/government/uploads/system/uploads/attachment_data/file/699810/School_inspection_handbook_section_5.pdf.

## Summary

Brede, J., Remington, A., Kenny, L., Warren, K. and Pellicano, L. (2016) *Back to School: Paving the Path to Re-integration for Autistic Children Previously Excluded from Education.* London: National Autistic Society.

Gore Langton, E. and Frederickson, N. (2015) 'Mapping the educational experiences of children with pathological demand avoidance.' *Journal of Research in Special Educational Needs 16,* 4, 254–263.

Gore Langton, E. and Syson, Z. (n.d.) *Simple Strategies for Supporting Children with Pathological Demand Avoidance at School.* Accessed on 19/04/2018 at www.pdasociety.org.uk/resources/education-resources/educational-strategies-booklet-from-positive-pda-2.

Jones, G., English, A., Guldberg, K., Jordan, R., Richardson, P. and Waltz, M. (2008) *Educational Provision for Children and Young People on the Autism Spectrum Living in England: A Review of Current Practice, Issues and Challenges.* London: Autism Education Trust.

O'Nions, E., Happé, F. and Viding, E. (2016) 'Extreme/"Pathological" demand avoidance.' *British Psychological Society DECP Debate,* issue 160.

Wittemeyer, K., Charman, T., Cusak, J., Guldberg, K., *et al.* (2011) *Educational Provision and Outcomes for People on the Autism Spectrum.* London: Autism Education Trust.

## Useful websites

Autism Education Trust (AET)
www.autismeducationtrust.org.uk

National Autistic Society (NAS)
www.autism.org.uk

PDA Society (PDA)
www.pdasociety.org.uk

# Index

curriculum personalisation
  designing 86–8
  official position on 85–6
  priorities for learning 88–91
  project-based curriculum 92–7
  reflections on 97–9

David, C. 10
Department of Children, Schools and
    Families (DCSF) 110
Department for Education (DfE) 85, 86,
    87, 131, 132
Department for Education and Skills
    (DfES) 110
Department of Health (DoH) 85, 86, 87,
    110, 132
developmental delay
  as characteristic of PDA 16
Diagnostic Interview for Social and
    Communication Disorders (DISCO)
    18
Diagnostic and Statistical Manual of
    Mental Disorders (DSM-IV) 10
distraction
  as teaching strategy 62
drama and role play
  as teaching strategy 58–9

E4L/SSAT 133
Education and Handling Guidelines for
    Children with PDA 31
Educational Provision and Outcomes for People
    on the Autism Spectrum (Wittemeyer) 86
Elizabeth Newson Centre 17
emotional regulation
  and AET Progression Framework 135
  as characteristic of PDA 14–15
emotional wellbeing
  and AET Progression Framework 134
  and flexibility 115
  and problem-solving 114
  promotion of 109–16
  as teaching strategy 67
  time for promoting 115–16
Engagement for Learning Framework 133
Every Child Matters (DfES) 110
expectations
  adjusting as teaching strategy 61–2
  recognition of 113

Extreme Demand Avoidance
  Questionnaire (EDA-Q) 17

families
  Collaborative Approaches to Learning
    37
  starting with a child with PDA 75–6,
    77
Faulconbridge, J. 110
Fidler, R. 123
flexibility
  as Collaborative Approaches to
    Learning principle 34–5
  and emotional wellbeing 115
  teaching implications 28–9
  as teaching strategy 50–1
Frederickson, N. 153

gender
  and research into PDA 18
Gilberg, Cristopher 17
Good Autism Practice (Christie) 31
Gore Langton, Emma 28, 153
Gould, Judy 17, 18

Happé, Francesca 11, 17
Hartley, David 87

impulsivity
  as characteristic of PDA 14–15
indirectness
  as teaching strategy 48–50
International Classification of Diseases
    (ICD-10) 10
invitational approach
  as teaching strategy 45–6

Jones, G. 152

language
  socially complex 51–2
Le Marechal, K. 10
learning implications of PDA
  anxiety of child with PDA 22
  meltdowns 23–4
  obsessions with other people 24–5

**Ruth Fidler** is an education consultant specialising in complex autism, pathological demand avoidance (PDA), interactive approaches and emotional wellbeing.

She worked at an all-age, non-maintained special school for 94 pupils across the autism spectrum for 22 years until 2014 and has worked independently since then. During her time on the senior leadership team the school sustained Ofsted outstanding status. Ruth worked within the school promoting interactive approaches and emotional wellbeing for pupils with complex autism. As a member of the leadership team she had a strategic role and contributed to continuing professional development for all staff. She also led an outreach pilot project working with other agencies to meet the needs of children and young people currently unable to attend school. She has experience of using music to promote interaction.

As well as providing training, she regularly observes and monitors teaching and learning, supporting staff to embed and refine good autism and SEND practice. She also regularly presents at local and national events and conferences for parents and a range of professionals. She provides training and consultancy for a variety of schools and parents and works all over the UK and with organisations including the Autism Education Trust, the National Autistic Society and the PDA Society. She is a member of the national Autism in Women and Girls Forum (www.naht.org.uk/about-us/our-councils-communities-and-forums/ autism-and-girls-forum) and the national PDA Development Group.

She has contributed to publications in the *Good Autism Practice (GAP)* journal on the subject of promoting emotional wellbeing and is co-author of two other books, *Understanding Pathological Demand Avoidance Syndrome in Children* (2012), and *Can I tell you about Pathological Demand Avoidance Syndrome?* (with Phil Christie; 2015), both published by Jessica Kingsley Publishers.

**Phil Christie** is a consultant child psychologist who established the Elizabeth Newson Centre (ENC) and now works on an independent basis. Phil was Director of Services and Principal of Sutherland House School for 30 years in addition to overseeing the ENC.

Phil has a particular specialism in pathological demand avoidance syndrome. PDA is a condition first described by Elizabeth Newson and is increasingly being recognised as part of the autism spectrum. Phil's work has also encompassed a range of activities such as training and research, which included an action research project on early diagnosis and intervention with 2–3-year-olds with autism. This project refined an approach known as 'Frameworks for Communication'.

For a number of years Phil was a team leader on the Autism Services Accreditation Programme, reviewing the quality of services for children with autism throughout the UK. Phil is an associate editor of *Good Autism Practice* and previously undertook the same role for *Autism: International Journal of Research and Practice*. He was elected as chair of the advisory council for the Autism Education Trust and is now vice-chair of the programme board. Phil has been involved in conferences, training sessions and presentations on a range of topics related to the autism spectrum across the UK and also in South Africa, Spain, Sweden, Holland, Finland, Romania, Ireland, Belgium and Greece. Over recent years Phil has been extensively involved in leading training events around PDA for schools and other organisations providing for children with complex presentations on the autism spectrum.

Phil has published widely in the field of autism and has co-authored a number of books on autism and PDA, including *First Steps in Intervention with your Child with Autism* (with Elizabeth Newson, Wendy Prevezer and Susie Chandler; 2009), *Understanding Pathological Demand Avoidance Syndrome in Children* (with Margaret Duncan, Ruth Fidler and Zara Healy; 2011), and *Can I tell you about Pathological Demand Avoidance Syndrome?* (with Ruth Fidler; 2015), all published by Jessica Kingsley Publishers.